ALLEN BREED SERIES

The Allen Breed Series examines horse and pony breeds from all over the world, using a broad interpretation of what a breed is: whether created by the environment where it originally developed, or by man for a particular purpose, selected for its useful characteristics, or for its appearance, such as colour. It includes all members of the horse family, and breeds with closed or protected stud books as well as breeds and types still developing.

Each book in the Allen Breed Series examines the history and development of the breed, its characteristics and use, and its current position in Britain, together with an overview of the breed in America and worldwide. More difficult issues are also tackled, such as particular problems associated with the breed, and such controversies as the effect of the show ring on working breeds. The breed societies and their role in modern breeding policies are discussed.

BOOKS IN THE SERIES

The Coloured Horse and Pony

Ridden champion at the 1990 British Skewbald and Piebald Association championships, Cinnebar II, owned and ridden by Mrs Christine Planton.

ALLEN BREED SERIES

The Coloured Horse and Pony

Edward Hart

J. A. Allen
London

British Library Cataloguing in Publication Data
A catalogue record for this book is available from the British Library

ISBN 0–85131–572–0

Published in Great Britain in 1993 by
J. A. Allen & Company Limited
1 Lower Grosvenor Place, London SW1W 0EL

Series editor Elizabeth O'Beirne-Ranelagh
Book production Bill Ireson
Printed in Great Britain by
St Edmundsbury Press Limited, Bury St Edmunds, Suffolk

To Audrey

Contents

Front cover: Boughton Penelope by the Thoroughbred Quality Fair, with her colt foal by Dallas Bright Spark.

Endpapers: Coloured horses belonging to the author's wife.

Acknowledgements

As there is no previous written history of British broken-coloured horses and ponies, I am more than usually indebted to the many owners who have talked to me. In addition to those whose words are quoted in the text, I am especially grateful to:

American Paint Horse Association; British Skewbald and Piebald Association; Coloured Horse and Pony Society of Great Britain; Painted Horse and Pony Society of Great Britain; Pinto Horse Association of New South Wales.

Ivan Armitage; Keith Chivers; Kate Elliott; Elwyn Hartley Edwards; Alan Harwood; Louella Stud; Tom Meagher; Susan Montgomery; Maridi Pletcher; John Porter; Sarah Porter; Clive Richardson; Tom Ryder; Eva Smith; The Lady Averil Swinfen; and a host of unnamed gypsies and travelling people.

Mike Scott BSc ARCS, Head of the Department of Immunology, Animal Health Trust, Newmarket, gave unsparingly of his specialist knowledge and time in helping shape the final chapter on genetics in layman's language (see pages 129–38). Carole Knowles-Pfeiffer kindly gave her permission to use an edited form of her research in chapters 3 (pages 25–33) and 10 (pages 124–9). Audrey Hart and Yvonne Johnson prepared the index.

The author and publishers are grateful to the following for permission to use photographs and illustrations:

American Paint Horse Association (page 30); British Skewbald and Piebald Association (frontispiece, pages 4, 8, 87); Coloured Horse and Pony Society (pages 78, 79, 80, 130, 131, 137); Eyre Methuen (pages 13, 15); Sally Mitchell Fine Arts (pages 70, 120, 121, 123); Louella Stud (pages 27, 74, 75); Chameleon Photography (page 98); John Bull Photography (frontispiece, pages 87, 128); Frank H. Meads (page 106); MVR Photographic (page 112); Pleasure Prints (page 80); Anthony Reynolds (page 83); Romany Gypsy Photograph Collection – Barry Law (pages 2, 59, 100); Kate Elliott (page 110); Jennifer Greaves (page 16); Audrey Hart (pages 6, 28 (bottom), 45, 50, 60, 61 (top), 66, 67, 68, 69, 92, 93, 97, 125, 132, 133, endpapers); Valerie Underwood (pages 3, 38); Diane Whiting (pages 11, 21, 82, 83, 85).

Introduction

The parti- or broken-coloured horse in Britain is in many ways like the lurcher dog. Both have been disregarded, even spurned, by generations of self-styled equine and canine authorities. Even those possessing such an animal might be suspect, the lurcher having poaching associations.

Then came the burgeoning realisation that here was something different. Brains and character became apparent even to those who previously 'didn't like that kind of thing'. The lurcher sprang into general and particularly *nouveau*-rural popularity, with lurcher shows staged far and wide and drawing enormous entries.

So with the parti-coloured horse. At one time it was exceptional to see one at a fashionable hunt meet; today the piebald or skewbald can command a premium. This merely reiterates the views of real countrymen and women who knew a good animal when they saw one, regardless of the views of the rest of the world. Born and reared among dogs and horses of all sizes, breeds, temperaments and crosses, they had noticed, without having to read about it first, that soundness, surefootedness, wearing ability and reliable temperament were often associated with the parti-coloured horse.

HM Queen Elizabeth II, with few peers for genuine horse knowledge, chooses parti-coloureds as drum horses for some of her regiments. Not only do they look imposingly magnificent, but they stand steadfast amongst the music, cheers and action of pageantry.

Ownership of a parti-coloured horse immediately gives entry to a world-wide brotherhood. Yet there are basic differences between British and American ideas. In Britain, parti-coloureds have often been derived from gypsy stock not many generations back. In North America, no draught blood is allowed in the Paint and Pinto registers, which roughly correspond with the Coloured Horse and Pony Society of Great Britain, the British Skewbald and Piebald Association, and latterly the Painted Horse and Pony Society of Great Britain.

American breeders impose their preferred colour patterns on a wide variety of types and breeds, mainly in the riding sphere. In Britain, there is more emphasis on the sound temperament and hard-wearing abilities associated with 'coloureds', characteristics which seem to be retained for a number of generations.

Another basic difference between the two sides of the Atlantic concerns terminology. In Britain, we have tended to cling to 'piebald' (white and black in fairly

1

Gypsy stock is often a source of British parti-coloured horses.

large, well-defined areas) and 'skewbald' (white and any colour other than black, i.e. chestnut, brown, bay or roan).

The Shorter Oxford English Dictionary lists 'piebald' as originating not later than 1589. It means 'of two different colours, esp. black and white (like the plumage of a magpie), usually arranged irregularly; pied, usually of animals, esp. horse'. The same source lists 'bald' as probably an Anglo-Saxon word meaning originally 'white patch'. It gives an alternative: 'streaked or marked with white (cf. Welsh *ceffyl bal.* French. *cheval belle-face*).'

Skewbald is defined by the Shorter Oxford as 'irregularly marked with white and brown or red, or some other colour'. The term was in use by the mid-seventeenth century, and may have had connections with the Old French word for a shield.

The rest of the world is usually much more precise in parti-coloured terminology, giving detailed classification and typing centred around the terms 'overo' and 'tobiano' (see pages 26–33). One of the main aims of this book is to encourage methodical and accurate recording of markings, which would in itself be a very real step forward in the realms of constructive breeding.

Basic questions are asked, and some answers given. Where the answer is unknown or debatable, I say so. The generally accepted laws of colour inheritance in horses, complicated enough in themselves for the lay person, are not always universally applicable to the parti-coloured horse.

Though matings to produce parti-colours are becoming better understood, there is still no way of forecasting or planning the *position* or *proportion* of the markings.

Two-month-old foal by Bee Alive (TB) out of a Cob/Thoroughbred cross. There is no way of telling from the parents what markings will appear on the foal.

Nor are there precise rules for keeping intense shades of black, bay, brown or chestnut, though breeders' experiences are passed on.

I hope that by the time the chapter on genetics is reached, readers' appetites will have been sufficiently whetted to tackle the groundwork of this intriguing subject. Application of a few basic principles may save disappointments; the breeding cycle of horses is so lengthy compared with their owners' practical horse-breeding span that any knowledge gained from science or past and present generations of breeders must be worthwhile.

Why coloureds?

'When the horse has ceased to be of use to mankind in one sphere, he is sure to be of service in another', wrote that influential horseman Sir Walter Gilbey around the turn of the century. One outlet almost a century after Sir Walter used those words is in the show jumping arena. Many competitors rely on a sponsor, and if a horse or pony is strikingly coloured *and* successful, its chances of attracting sponsorship rise quite sharply.

Katherine Lilley, successfully competing on her 14.2 hands Blaze in showing, show jumping and cross country.

An obviously sound temperament in a cob-type competitor.

Show organisers depend much on entrance money to keep their societies thriving. The paying public seeks something with which it can easily identify. A series of classes of immaculate middle and heavyweight hunters, mostly bays, chestnuts and a few greys and blacks, can become boring for most ringside viewers.

The coloureds are easy to distinguish and compare, even by the tyro. Parents with young children can amuse their offspring by pointing out the different markings, and guessing which will gain the coveted rosette. Here is one very big 'plus' in favour of the coloured horse, and one that show secretaries are beginning to recognise.

Lostock Blue, champion stallion and winner of hunter and working hunter classes, shown competing at the Nottinghamshire County show.

Racehorse trainers appreciate the value of a handy mount quite unmistakable from the string on the gallops. A suitable piebald or skewbald is more and more in demand for this purpose. He needs both a turn of speed and a placid character, quite happy to stand when his rider needs to watch carefully from a static position, as is often the case.

When the 1991 European Three-Day Event championships were staged at Punchestown, Ireland, the dozen or so marshalls were splendidly mounted on active

Presenting a petition to 10 Downing Street during the campaign for Minimum Values on exported horses and ponies.

Badger, owned and driven by Bernard Hunt, appeared in the Lord Mayor's New Year's Day parade in London in 1991. He is seen here harnessed to a closed Clarence owned by the Lancashire Carriage Collection.

coloured horses. This really was impressive. Like cricket umpires wearing dark trousers against the players' white flannels, these marshalls were readily distinguishable. What happens when more and more coloureds actually compete may be left to the future.

Ireland has a great selection of such high-class animals, for a rather curious reason. Racing stables there are using coloured mares as nurses for Thoroughbred foals. These mares not only have ample milk but, more important, a strong maternal temperament that allows them to take on a strange foal easily, sometimes in addition to their own. It is of course essential that these nurse mares are in milk to coincide with the Thoroughbred foaling calendar. To be so they must bear a foal, and what more obvious than to put them to the readily available blood stallions?

Even after a few generations it seems that the coloureds' maternal and milking abilities remain unimpaired.

Dr Tom Meagher, a practising vet in County Tipperary, writes:

Of the coloured horses, the most common are black and white piebald, commonly referred to here as the 'Battie'. These were originally only kept by the Travelling Community, and were not then very highly thought of by others.

The Travelling Community kept them mainly as a means of cheap transport, but because of their ability to reproduce prolifically, it was not long before they had large numbers. Most of these 'Batties' were around 14 hands high, and it was quite rare to see larger horses. Other colours, red/white 'Skewbalds' and blue/white, were less common. Nowadays the situation has completely changed, and it is very fashionable to have coloured horses in all sports from show jumping, eventing, polo to hunting. The more colour the better.

In the television and film industries, parti-coloured horses can make an unsurpassable spectacle. Ridden at full gallop across rugged terrain in Arizona, or standing statue-still as the wagon train winds below, they have thrilled generations of Western fans. For close-ups, however, they have one major drawback. Most coloured horses are readily recognised, even by non-horsey people. They can thus be used only in one general area, or with one particular vehicle. This adds to the film company's costs, for substitutions become impractical.

A dozen blacks and bays may be hired, and filmed drawing a stage coach with outriders. The same horses then line a hitching rail in a town supposedly 30 miles away, and no eyebrows are raised. Had some of these horses been strikingly marked piebalds, then this harmless deception would not have succeeded, and extra horses would be needed.

A Red Indian chief, gaily bedecked in bright headdress, looks doubly magnificent mounted on an upstanding skewbald. That same horse is so eye-catching that it can never be used as an 'extra' in the film, whereas a whole-coloured animal might well play a 'bit' part in addition. Here is one occasion when the parti-coloured's very individuality works against it.

2 The mists of time

The earliest records of coloured horses come from cave drawings. In southern France and Spain these are an estimated 20,000 years old, and at Teyjat a cave drawing depicts a speckled mare and foal and a parti-coloured pony. These 'painted' horses, piebalds and skewbalds, trace back to pre-history, and are found in India, Tibet, Russia and all over Europe.

Homer mentioned Parthian cavalry horses, pure white with large deep bay spots and a gentle nature. Virgil alluded to the Borghese breed of pied horses near Rome, which appeared in the Trojan games. They were still being bred in the same locality in 1841.

In *The World's Best Horse* (1958), Lady Wentworth states: 'At the Rupture of the Duke of Mareb, AD 120, the King of Yemen took refuge in Syria with 80,000 parti-coloured Arab horses; and the Caliph Motassem, AD 840, had a stud of 130,000 spotted, speckled and dappled Arabian horses of the type seen in the Persian MS.' She claims that skewbalds were common in Spanish horses in the Middle Ages. She continues:

> Parti-colours of every conceivable pattern and shade are traditional in North Africa, and even in Arabian history. The Tanghans of Tibet had magnificent rainbow colouration, from which the Kathiawar got every variety of spots, speckles, splashes, and the oddest streaks, stripes and patches, including blue and green edgings. In the Himalayas a tiny breed of ten-hand skewbald ponies were observed by d'Hobsonville, wiry, active, fiery, and covered with regular coloured spots.

One Arab horse for whose picture the artist had to use seven different colours is recorded by Lady Wentworth. The poet El Arifi wrote glowingly in AD 1530 of the skewbald Arabians in the Royal stables of the Kings of Persia after the Arab conquest. They were seen in Persian miniatures as typical orientals with large eyes, crested neck and high tail carriage.

'When he spurs his wind-footed skewbald thou mightest say he mingles fire with wind', wrote El Arifi of the king's skewbald Arabian when playing a ball game. 'The horse of the King in galloping bore away the ball; he sprang from plain to plain like a ball.' 'If he had not been restrained in his leaping he would have outrun the ball.' 'He passed down the mountain like a torrent. Going forth to ball play with his Arab horse – Water could not keep pace with him nor the wind catch up with the dust he raised.'

Lady Wentworth tells us further:

> Abbas Pasha had a parti-coloured Wadneh Hursanieh mare by a Shueyman Sbah sire called Tabbukh belonging to Mohammed Ibn Khubeysan. She originated with Hamoud Saadun Sheik of the Muntaghaj, and was great-granddam of Mahruss I. It is from her that the white patches seen in some of our horses such as Nezma Shareer, Astrella, and Sharina are probably inherited. I have just received photographs of a pure Arab mare, Trabag, first prize at Palermo Show 1949, lavishly skewbald in irregular patterns, chestnut and white, and tracing back to the Crabbet horse Ajman. She has a white mane and tail.

As long ago as c. AD 750 Abu Bekr listed a whole range of Arabian colour varieties including creamy russet, with black mane and tail, and black down the back.

This horse, found working in a riding school in Tangiers, was said to be a pure-bred Arab. No one could explain his colouring.

Parti-coloured Arabs listed by Abu Obeyda include white with coloured head and neck or vice versa; both ends white with piebald body; speckled with spots of the same size all over; and 'Adjnaf', bay or black stomach, and the rest any other colour. 'Mulemma' was spotted, while 'Anbat' described white legs right up in the body, possibly including the belly. Ears and forelock bay, the rest skewbald or piebald, was another category. 'Ashal' in Arabic denoted a horse with white back and ash-coloured body. Chestnuts and bays with large white patches were also found, while 'Abrash' described small spots in either black or white, or with white spots like a leopard, or a variety of coloured spots and stripes.

An attendant to Sir T. Roe in East India, writing in 1615, is quoted by Lady Wentworth: 'This Empire further affords . . . horses limned for their colours raven black but many more white curiously dappled and a very great number pied and spotted all over, and there are some of other bright colours.' Their riders 'manage their horses with strong snaffles, whose reins and head-stalls are made suitable to their saddles and trappings'.

All over the Orient, horses with distinguishing broken colours date back to pre-history. Spotted horses are found in Chinese art dated 500 BC, and in AD 960 in Persian art. From AD 618 onwards, oriental statues and paintings feature skew-balds and piebalds, and by the fourteenth century they were common in Spanish art.

Cortez took 'raindrop' horses with him during the invasion of Mexico in the early sixteenth century. The acute observations of Bernal Diaz del Castillo on the different colours that were to help found American equine history are of great interest to students of colour. Horses were scarce and expensive in Cuba, from which base the Mexican expedition embarked, and it was only with great difficulty that any were procured.

Among a number of bays, greys and chestnuts was a piebald horse, inclining to black in the markings, with white forefeet, which turned out to be worthless. Moron of Vaimo, however, bought a piebald with white feet and a very good mouth.

This small group of horses, the first to land on the New World mainland, was so stiff after the sea voyage that they could hardly move. Yet the survivors had an influence beyond what could have been conjectured at the time. Some were set free or escaped, and were captured by indigenous tribes.

High-school riding – haute-école – was popular among eighteenth-century Spanish aristocrats, and soon spread to the rest of Europe. The nobility could seek and afford the cream of the horse population over a fairly wide area of North Africa and the Continent, and they chose a surprisingly high proportion of piebalds and skewbalds.

This is proven in *The Classical Riding Master*, an illustrated book on the Wilton House Collection for which the 10th Earl of Pembroke commissioned 35 gouache pictures. Commentary is by the late Dorian Williams, one of the mid-twentieth century's most knowledgeable horsemen, and he wrote: 'It is worth noting that

An illustration from *The Classical Riding Master*, showing a skewbald horse in a half turn on the haunches to the right.

many of the horses depicted come from countries that were part of the Hapsburg Empire – Hungary, Moravia, Silesia, Bohemia.' Later he adds: 'It is interesting, too, to observe the different types of horses used as models for the pictures. The Arab, the Thoroughbred, the chunky English horse, the powerful, compact Andalusian: and all colours, including skewbalds.'

A skewbald demonstrates the half turn to the right. 'It is interesting and, one would have thought, unusual to find these piebalds and skewbalds on the Continent in the eighteenth century', commented Dorian Williams.

The artist is Baron Reis d'Eisenberg, a renowned Riding Master in the Court of the Hapsburgs under Charles VI and Francis I. The high-school movements depicted are absolutely correct, so we may be sure that the colours are faithful also.

A strikingly vivid piebald is chosen to show the correct seat for a classical horseman, with the long stirrup of the dressage seat resulting in the rider's near straight leg. The croupade is demonstrated by a chestnut-and-white horse, while the ballotade to the left and then to the right also show coloured horses, one being depicted on the cover of the book.

Lord David Stuart, in *An Illustrated History of Belted Cattle* (1970), which deals with many classes of livestock, looks at the history of breeding coloured horses.

> As far as I am aware, no one has attempted to breed belted horses, unless the Chinese have done so in the past; yet they do occur from time to time, chiefly among ponies in this country. In Lord Macartney's account of his embassy to China, in the years 1793–4, he records having seen belted horses, along with many piebald, spotted and roan animals, at the Summer Palace, in Jehol. The late Group-Captain H. St Clair Smallwood, who knew Inner and Outer Mongolia well, told me that horses of every conceivable colour were to be found there and that he had often seen them belted.

Lord David lists some of the wild species of birds and mammals where belting occurs, including the Malaysian tapir, the Giant Panda, the sea piet, the avocet, the hoodie crow and the rose-coloured starling. Among domesticated birds are the Lakenvelder hen and the Lahore pigeon. Among domesticated animals belting occurs in cattle, goats, pigs, horses, mice, rats, guinea pigs and rabbits.

Thus there is much evidence of parti-coloured horses before written history, but how did they arise in the first place? Professor J. Cossar Ewart, Regius Professor of Natural History, University of Edinburgh, wrote in 1910: 'Even in prehistoric times

The correct seat of the horsemen from *The Classical Riding Master*.

domestic animals varied. That they began to vary very soon after they were first domesticated is clearly shown by recent explorations in central Asia.'

Professor Ewart said that the stability of a species is disturbed by domestication, when in addition to artificial selection there is an almost complete cessation of natural selection. This has led to the most striking fact about modern breeds of domestic animals, that they consist of strains which often differ in form, colour and disposition.

'Changes in conformation, colour, coat and horns doubtless attracted quite as much attention in prehistoric times as they do today.' wrote Professor Ewart. When

Piebald is a typical colour amongst Icelandic horses. Jennifer Greaves' French-bred Titou.

experimenting with zebras he found that the wild striped horses of Africa differed among themselves in form, size and markings, and were specialised for different habitats.

Most authorities believe that modern horse breeds had a multiple origin, and that among their ancestors were included 'steppe', 'desert' and 'forest' types. We can today see the onager's distinct lighter shading on its belly and flanks, and will see later how roan can throw a variety of odd colours. Thus we can at least conjecture on how the remote ancestors of our present beloved broken colours could have arisen.

In 1917 Professor Cosser Ewart wrote a Foreword to *Horses*, by Roger Pocock, who describes himself as 'an old rough-neck of the American ranges'. Pocock worked among horses in many countries, and in his opinion true black was unknown among outdoor horses, and could only be due to special selective breeding.

On colour origins he also has his own ideas:

The primary horse colours are Dun and Bay.

The secondary colours are white, black, chestnut and brown.

The tertiary colours are crosses of white with Bay, Dun, black, chestnut, brown which produce the various roans.

The quarternary colours are crosses of white with whole roans, producing strawberry and cream roans, and roan-balds; while a peculiar mixture of white with black, bay or chestnut gives us the piebalds and skewbalds.

The white horse, says Pocock, has been saved from the wolves by man, but the secondary, tertiary and quarternary colours are also very largely the result of crossing the primitive strains of Europe with the imported African Bay within the last couple of thousand years.

In *Bridleways through History*, published in 1948, Lady Viola Apsley broaches the subject of colour in equine history. 'No doubt a great deal depends today on fashions – as, for instance, the prevalence in eighteenth-century Germany for curiously marked, spotted and piebald riding horses – fashionable also in Ancient China.'

She remarks that colour characteristics are 'so far only vaguely understood and very controversial'. More than forty years later, the mysteries have certainly not all been solved.

Lady Apsley quotes some pertinent observations on skin colour from Professor Starling of London University.

Northern white-skinned horses will not survive in the tropics, where white-haired, black-skinned horses thrive much better – a fact equally true of cattle, pigs and dogs. It seems that all animals indigenous to the tropics have black skins to evaporate internal heat, and a light coat to protect them against the sun's rays – also a protection against snow glare in the Arctic and high regions.

So in the case of animals in the tropics that have to be abroad in daytime, Nature usually provides them with lighter coloured tawny or white hairs above their black skin. True Arabian horses invariably have black skins.

The oldest cave drawings of horses some hundred thousand years ago suggest a roan – which, like a modern chestnut, reflects heat in summer and conserves it in winter.

White-faced horses, says Lady Apsley, were much admired by the Greeks as evidence of a new infusion of better blood. 'White and black horses are likewise mentioned as being highly prized – and these colours come from a first cross of the "Arabian type" on "Asiatic" breeds.'

Although the early Scandinavian horses were mostly dun-coloured, claims Lady Apsley, the god Heimdal in Norse mythology rode a yellow-maned horse called 'Gold-topped', while Raven and Sooty were among names at an early date, showing that black horses were already known. 'For the most part, down to modern times, duns, piebalds and greys remain typical colours of Scandinavian horses.'

As we shall see, with the beginning of organised breeding many societies outlawed coloured horses and ponies in their studbooks. But the colour persisted and still crops up to this day.

Colours, markings and terminology

The base colours

In North America, the agricultural colleges made far greater impact in equine studies in the first quarter of the twentieth century than their equivalents in the UK. Horse husbandry was studied more systematically, and the results of such matters as the draught required per implement, and the means of yoking large teams of horses to achieve it, were passed on to practical horsemen of field or prairie. When Lippincott's Farm Manuals were produced, before World War I, there were twenty-one million horses in the USA.

In 1913, Carl W. Gay, Professor of Animal Husbandry at the University of Minnesota, wrote *Productive Horse Husbandry* in the Lippincott series, and put economic efficiency as his main plank. To this end he stressed: 'Certain colours are preferred or even required in some classes of horses where other colours are undesirable or even prohibited.' His conclusions help the modern breeder of coloured horses, as they specify the pros and cons of the different colours, with the proviso that he wrote primarily for a country with higher summer temperatures than the UK. He pointed out:

> Colour is the most conspicuous feature by which a horse can be described or identified, so that a uniform and comprehensive colour standard is important. Colours may be generally classed as solid or broken, distinguished by the presence or absence of white spots. Solid colours are further differentiated as hard or soft. A hard colour is one in which the shade is sharply pronounced, while soft colours are characterised by either a total absence of pigment, as in the case of white horses with pink skins, or a washed-out or faded shade of some of the other colours.
>
> Broken colours are either the piebald and skewbald, in which the amount of white is considerable and the distribution irregular; or marked, when the white is limited in amount and definitely restricted in its location.
>
> Then there are a number of odd colours and markings which do not conform to the above distinctions nor admit of any but a group classification.

Gay quoted stud-book studies and observations on how colours behave in transmission. It is interesting to remember that his 1920 and 1924 revised editions coincided with a peak of registrations in the British Clydesdale and Shire stud books, amply sufficient numbers to monitor. Shire entries in Volume 41 (1920) totalled 6043, and included 816 stallions. Clydesdales in 1920 amassed 6870 entries.

Gay's main conclusions were that 'chestnut is recessive to all other colours, black is dominant to chestnut and recessive to all others, bay is dominant to chestnut and black and recessive to roan, grey and dun; roan appears to be a pattern independent of the kind of pigment and dominant to all other colours.' This last conclusion he bases on E. Wentworth's *Color Inheritance in the Horse* (1914).

Carl Gay's views on how the different colours are considered raise some very valid points. Bay he regards as 'everyman's' colour, with brown also a good all-round colour.

> Chestnut, especially the golden and red, is one of the most attractive colours and when accompanied by white markings, as chestnut is liable to be, presents an extremely flashy appearance . . .
>
> Black, while most popular in fiction, is in fact not a good colour for selling. It is objected to chiefly on the ground that it is not often fast black but fades and sunburns badly in hot weather; the sooty more so than the jet black. Black is also objectionable on account of the flecked appearance which it acquires as the horse is warmed up. No matter how carefully the coat is groomed, every hair that is turned appears as a dirty, grey fleck, as soon as the sweat dries. Black harness horses are commonly cross-matched with greys . . .
>
> Grey is the colour most in demand in the draft classes . . . they experience less difficulty in matching up a team of from two to six greys than in the case of any other colour . . . It would seem at first thought that bays could be more easily matched than greys. But bays are frequently marked with white, which necessitates a matching of markings as well as of shade. Greys, furthermore, appear to harmonize better with the red, green, or yellow combinations in which most commercial vehicles are finished. It is also reasonable to claim that the grey horse is less sensitive to heat than the horse of darker colour, since white has the physical property of reflecting the sun's rays, while black absorbs them.
>
> Grey horses . . . are generally objected to because of the conspicuousness of their hair when shed; the degree in which they show stable stain.

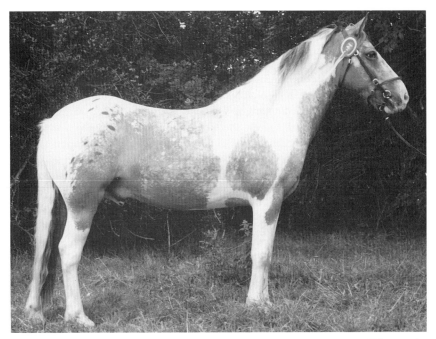

Unusual markings showing parti-colour, roaning and Appaloosa-type spots. Whereas the body colour is brown, there is black in both the mane and tail.

The last comments also apply to the piebald or skewbald with a large proportion of white.

'Piebald and skewbald are popular colours in ponies, and in sporting fours and tandems where striking colours are a feature', said Carl Gay. They were also sought after 'for advertising wagons and the circus, where it is desirable to have them conspicuous'.

Gay agreed with the common wisdom that white markings added to the appearance of a flashy show horse. But his opinion was that any white markings should be as symmetrical as possible and sharply defined, wherever they occurred.

21

Carl Gay perhaps added to the confusion in the USA concerning the characteristic colour of the Arab. He said:

> Almost any odd colour or marking, such as pure white, piebald, skewbald, leprous or tiger spots, are attributed to Arab blood. Such significance of any of these colours has been absolutely denied. While the odd colours referred to as suggesting Arab breeding are never found among pure bred Arabs, they are noted among their half breeds, the piebalds and skewbalds, especially, occurring with a considerable degree of uniformity when the common stock of Upper Asia and Europe is crossed with Arab sires. This is shown in the piebald ponies of Tibet, Sumatra, Iceland, the Faroe Islands, Java, India, and our original American range ponies, which were not many generations removed from Oriental foundation.

However, as we have seen, all the colours and markings he mentions have at some time or other been found in pure Arabs.

The white markings

Piebald and skewbald horses are not found among today's registered Arabian or Thoroughbred horses, as the colours have been long banned in their stud books. The world-famous Italian racehorse breeder Frederico Tesio points out in *Breeding the Racehorse* (1958) that:

> Practically all wild animals and birds have coloured markings on their coats and their feathers. At times these markings are white, like those of the horse. But in wild animals they are always symmetrical . . . Penguins, for instance, all have black backs and white fronts, with the white front exactly centred like a carefully worn dress shirt. I have seen them in groups of thousands in the Tierra del Fuego, looking for all the world like expectant waiters in a huge restaurant. The stripes of the tiger's coat are always symmetrical on both sides of the body and the zebra has a slightly different design but it too is symmetrical and constant throughout the breed. Instead in the thoroughbred, a hybrid, the markings are not symmetrical. On the foreheads of many thoroughbreds, for example, we find white spots known as stars. These stars, like comets, often have a tail trailing down toward the nose. In some instances this tail

22

swerves abruptly to one side, as if the brush had slipped from the painter's hand.

This is seen in many breeds of horse. The white socks of a Shire or Clydesdale (both hybrids, whatever the breed societies may claim!) vary from nil to well above the knee or, more usually, above the hock. The great Clydesdale stallion Dunure

White face and extensive white leg markings on Bobby, belonging to Bill and Karen Hedges of Kent.

Footprint had a light roan patch on his near side, but after he became famous, and successful at stud, he was always photographed from the other side!

These markings have intrigued horsemen since horsemanship began:

> If your horse has four white socks, keep him not a day;
> If your horse has three white socks, send him far away;
> If your horse has two white socks, sell him to a friend;
> If your horse has one white sock, keep him to the end!

Another version reads:

> One white sock, buy him;
> Two white socks, try him;
> Three white socks, lend him;
> Four white socks, send him.

This is not adhered to by modern Shire breeders, who seek black or bay with four white socks as the epitome of showring perfection. The appearance of one coloured leg 'spoils' the horse for the brewery team or trade turnout. I was once asked by a well-known bank to find a black heavy horse with four black legs. Not only could I find no such heavy, but breeders wouldn't believe such an animal was wanted!

Beliefs concerning colour are full of contradictions. Tesio quotes from a book by G. B. Trutta published in Naples in 1699:

> Horses with white hind feet are of greater value than those with white on the fore-feet, inasmuch as these last are less vigorous. If the horse has three white legs he is considered fit for a King, for he is sure to be of excellent quality. If all four feet are white and the horse also has white in his face, he will be of gentle disposition, but of scant success in action. The horse with a white mark on his right hind foot ... is to be avoided, for horses thus marked are disastrous in their performance ...

Tesio describes these sayings as 'like a portrait with the outline drawn from life, but coloured by superstition. He claims that 'horses with large white markings are less energetic than others, and more susceptible to afflictions of the skin on their white legs'.

He has his own theories about how parti-colours first arose.

> When 'homo sapiens' of prehistoric times first attempted to cross a mare of pure albino blood [i.e. with skin totally lacking in pigment] with a stallion of bay or chestnut ancestry, he awaited with curiosity the birth of the first hybrid and it seemed perfectly natural to him when the colt was born a piebald.

Despite his reservations about parti-coloureds, Tesio adds:

> There were, however, two centuries in which the fashion of the day brought about a revival of the piebald. In the 16th and 17th centuries, under the influence of Asiatic splendour and Spanish pomp, this type of horse was considered particularly decorative in parades and military celebrations.

Terminology for coloured horses

A totally dedicated student of coat colours, Carole Knowles-Pfeiffer, has brought the classification of colour in the pied horse to a fine art. She is a graduate of the University of Wales, where she lectured in Equine Studies (a post-graduate course). She has worked for some thirty years with breeders and breed societies world-wide. In the USA, she was for many years a qualified inspector for the Pinto Horse Association of America. In Britain, she used to advise the original Coloured Horse and Pony Society about studbook acceptances and on breeding for colour generally. She has also been involved with a breeding programme to produce pied drum horses at the Royal Paddock since about 1975. Her work is the basis of the following explanations.

In Britain, we are familiar with the terms 'piebald' and 'skewbald'. *Piebald* is black and white in patches, while *skewbald* is technically any other colour than black together with white patches. In fact skewbald is usually thought to be *red* and white, and this may be a brown, bay or chestnut base colour. In reality, *any* base colour you can think of – such as dun, palomino, roan or whatever – together with white patches constitutes skewbald. Both piebald and skewbald may go grey, then white. But they are still pied under the greying factor.

In America, both North and South, and in many other English-speaking countries, a fairly simple 'pied' terminology not yet familiar in Britain is used virtually exclusively. Interestingly, it is based on Latin-American Spanish, with more recent additions in English for some special patterns of pied. It seems logical to have a universally accepted language for the various colours and patterns of broken-coloured horses, though in reality, a common language for the *base* colour would be less easy to create than colour/white pattern terminology.

The Americans have long held the parti-coloured horse in high esteem and have founded various registries for such animals. These societies have affiliated bodies in many other countries including Australia, New Zealand and South Africa. Slowly, the 'American' terminology is becoming the most universally accepted, which is why the reader should be familiar with it.

Tobiano

All the US registries use the terms 'tobiano' and 'overo'. Let us examine *tobiano* first, since this is a familiar pied in Britain. *Tobiano* is a Latin-American Spanish word. To look at, it is a basic (but much varied) pattern of white body markings on *any* base colour. The characteristic feature of the tobiano pattern is that the white is *dorsal*, or top-of-the-animal in origin. The best way to explain it is to imagine that you start off with a solid base-colour horse and two pots of white paint. One pot of white is poured down the lower neck/shoulder region and the other over the rump. You can then imagine that the paint 'runs' down the sides of the animal. This will tend to leave a dark head, chest and flanks. The boundaries between the white and the colour are sharply defined. The dorsal (spinal) line is very rarely wholly dark, quite the reverse. Head white is not normally extensive and any present is much as on a solid-colour horse. However dark the animal may be, one can expect to see white leg markings like stockings on three or all legs, but in many cases the legs are virtually totally white. The tail may be dark, white or a mix.

As with all 'pieds', the tobiano may be almost completely dark, with just one or two small areas of white in the dorsal region, and white stockings on the legs; or it may be almost totally white with a dark head. Neither of these is the norm. Interestingly, the extreme white extensions of all pieds is a horse with some colour remaining at the top of the head and on the ears. This is called the 'war-bonnet'. There is usually more white on the overo than on the tobiano head.

Even though the tobiano is common in Britain, it is now banned in most breed registeries; only the Shetland Pony Society allows the pattern to be registered. How, then, can it be so common? The answer is quite simple. Like grey, the tobiano is basically a very easy pattern to introduce into any breed by crossing. The

Clear tobiano markings on Samona, a Dutch Warmblood stallion belonging to the Louella Stud.

factor for this pied is said to be *dominant*, in other words it acts over and above the factor for non-pied, so that a parent showing this pattern can be expected to pass it on to at least fifty per cent of its foals where the other parent is solid coloured. That is how it can so easily be infused into pure breeds, especially by crossing to pure females, and by selecting the pied cross. By breeding back to the pure breed again and once more selecting the pied foal, one can establish a new purebred type – of pied pattern – in a few generations. For breeders with some knowledge and imagination, the possibilities for producing superb quality tobianos of every conceivable type is endless. This kind of pied is far easier to breed for than any other pied or spotting characteristic.

Extremes of colour: minimal body white on a bay tobiano (*above*) and (*below*) minimal colour on the top of the head and on the flanks of two tobianos.

Overo

Horses and ponies registered as *overo* may not be so familiar, *nor in some cases even regarded as pied*. But pieds they certainly are. They can vary greatly, but they have two vital characteristics in common. The first and more important is that the white is *ventral* in origin. This means that it appears to come from the bottom of the animal, rather than from the top, as in tobiano. The second characteristic is that these pieds may well not have a pied parent, and can, and frequently do, cause great consternation by appearing with no warning from parents with no history of pied or excess white markings – even in pure breeds!

This sort of pied is known as a *crop-out*. Sensible societies who ban pieds record them and redirect them to the correct registries. Others try to pretend that they never existed and too often cast them quietly out of the back door.

It should be noted that while many of these ventral overo pieds in America are obviously different, many seem to be a mix and are difficult to define. This is not surprising in a country where pieds are liked and selected for. One is rather 'in the dark' breeding overos, and too often and maybe by accident, pieds from possible different genetic sources have been interbred. In Europe, the different patterns have tended to remain much more clear cut and easier to classify.

Carole Knowles-Pfeiffer has drawn up her own classification of overos. The most famous and 'classic' definition of *overo* she renamed the *frame* overo. These simply stunning pieds do not seem to occur in Europe. Could they be a mutation that has occurred in America? William F. (Buffalo Bill) Cody's Wild West Show, travelling Europe and America in the late 1880s, had many of these superb pieds. They are described by a contemporary writer as follows:

> This animal gives every appearance of being a dark based horse with white patches that seem to originate in the belly region and radiate outwards. The white tends to be much more broken and jagged-edged than white of tobianos and it appears mostly along the middle area of the horse from the top of the neck and into the hindquarters. Because the legs are mainly dark, and white very rarely crosses the back line, this gives the effect of the most beautifully arranged white markings bordered by a dark frame. The tail is normally dark and it is not unusual to have a lot of head white, and by that I mean a 'bald' white head is not uncommon. The eyes may be blue in this case.

TOBIANO

OVERO

Typical patterns of tobiano and overo, as published by the American Paint Horse Association. The Association gives the following general identification guide:

Tobiano
1. Head marked like a solid-coloured horse (either solid or will have blaze, stripe, star or snip).
2. Generally all four legs will be white, or at least white below the hocks and knees.
3. Spots are usually regular and distinct, often coming in oval or round patterns that extend down over the neck and chest giving the appearance of a shield.
4. Horse will usually have the dark colour on one or both flanks.
5. Horse may be either predominantly dark or white.

Overo
1. White will rarely cross the back between the withers and the tail.
2. Generally, at least one, and often all four, legs will be the dark colour.
3. Head markings will often be bald, apron or even bonnet-faced.
4. Irregular, rather scattered or splashy white markings on the body, often referred to as calico patterns.
5. Tail is usually one colour.
6. Horse may be either predominantly dark or white.

It is Mrs Knowles-Pfeiffer's opinion that this pattern is most seen in horses of stock type, and she has never yet seen one of European breeding. Some may have a lot of white, but generally they are dark. These seem to be rarer today, maybe because, in breeding for overos, other patterns have been introduced. This would result in more leg white for a start. Another interesting observation is that the 'lethal white' foal has never been recorded in Europe. These foals are born white and are thought to be linked to the overo pattern. They are born with abnormal nerves in the large gut and cannot survive as the gut is static at that point. One

Frame overo, showing the more irregular edges to the pattern which is common in overos.

wonders if this effect is in some way linked to the frame overo, but that is a theory based purely on observation.

Next comes the *splashed white* overo. They have to be classed as overo because they are registered as such. They are *so* rare that few people have even seen one, and those who do confuse them with tobiano. These pieds are almost invariably *crop-outs*; they do not breed true and are very difficult to reproduce to order. To look at they resemble a negative black and white image of the tobiano. In reality they have a white head, white chest and white flanks. The white is in large patches with clear-cut edges. The legs are normally extensively white, and white often crosses the backline. A distinctive feature is the absolutely bald-white head and blue eyes, though rarely the eye may be silver. The animal looks like a white base horse that has had colour poured on to it from the top. Over a period of some twenty years Mrs Knowles-Pfeiffer has made an in-depth study of *splashed whites*, but feels she is not much wiser, in spite of probably having seen more than any other living person. Fortunately for her, breeders have had accurate records and allowed her to study them at length, which has given her a possible reason for *how* they occur, but not the genetic cause.

Finally comes the *sabino* which makes up most of the registered *overos*, though the British may not consider some of the variations of sabino to be pied at all. They are quite common in numerous breeds, especially those that allow liberal white head and leg markings. This said, there could be a genetic link. The variations of sabino are endless, but there is a basic pattern. At least they are horses or ponies with high leg white, often up and over the knees in front and the hocks and/or the stifle behind. The white edges are always very broken, feathery or even spotted. The flanks may be flecked or spotted white as may be the chest. Belly white in varying amounts from a small area to a huge area is common, as is extensive head white. However, one thing is interesting; the white does not usually surround the eyes. This area and the cheeks are normally dark. Only in extreme white extension is the head bald white (or if mixed with another pied). Sometimes the animal is very heavily roaned, but in a way different from Appaloosa roaning or the dominant roan coat. It is a sort of mottled roan. The ultimate white extension is the viable *whiteborn*, but these usually have some colour, even if only on the ears and perhaps along the dorsal line, or as skin spots. *Whiteborns* mated to solids frequently produce sabino pieds. All sabinos throw a variety of pieds – with and without roaning. The truth is you just don't know what to expect with this pied. It is not difficult to find, but to establish it as a predictably marked breeder is virtually impossible. It is common in the Clydesdale, the Thoroughbred, the Arab, the Welsh breeds and many others, and it seems to be on the increase. It cannot be said to be a simple dominant gene, but sometimes it may be seen to be. Mrs Knowles-Pfeiffer believes that there is a basic pattern factor that depends for its great variability on numerous other genes for white and/or spotting. This is the only sensible way to explain the great variety of 'patterns' that constitute or result from sabino. In America, virtually every sort from one with the smallest amount of belly white to the most mottled roan can be registered as an overo.

Other classifications

US authors Sponenberg and Beaver have identified additional classifications, including rabicano, a pattern occurring in many breeds including Arab, Quarter Horse, Welsh and Hackney. Its extent may be so slight that the pattern is missed,

Rabicano markings on a partbred Quarter Horse yearling.

and it is usually not included in colour descriptions. It may consist of only a few white hairs, normally on the flanks and at the base of the tail. Horses with a more extensive pattern are flecked from the flanks extending outwards, between the front and hind legs and more heavily at the base of the tail. Such horses may be confused with roan, but there is a distinctive difference.

A classification that could only be American is termed 'skunk tail', also 'frosty' or 'silvery'. It is an unusual pattern, a little like rabicano. In addition to white hairs at the base of the tail and in the mane, there are white hairs in the spinal region and over other bony protuberances, such as the hocks and the pelvic bones. Sponenberg and Beaver suggest that it is this pattern, in addition to roan, that is responsible for the roan manes and tails on roan horses such as the Brabants.

Medicine hat paint or war bonnet paint are terms for similar patterns, where a mainly white horse will have colour on the ears, and possibly ears and eyes, and in the case of 'medicine hat' coloured patches on the chest, flank and base of tail. This is not a separate pattern, like overo or tobiano, but a description of a particular form which these patterns can take. Sponenberg and Beaver tell us that 'The patch on the ears is considered the "bonnet" and the body patches are like "war shields".' They go on to say that 'Horses with these markings were thought by some tribes of American Indians to be imbued with supernatural powers.' Stock people everywhere and throughout the ages have tended to associate special markings with certain attributes of physique and temperament, however disproved by modern genetic science.

Colour in breeds around the world

Europe

Some pure breeds around the world do accept parti-colours in their stud books, and others used to do so. Some of them are described in this chapter. Even where piebalds and skewbalds are accepted, they seldom affect the name, but the Piebald Pottock is an exception. It is a French pony, varying between 11.1 and 13 hands high. We should probably also call it skewbald, as bay, brown and chestnut base colours are also found. Piebald Pottocks may be black and white, black/chestnut and white, or chestnut and white.

A bay and white Piebald Pottock has a black mane and tail, and black above the white socks. In his native Basque mountain region he is a sturdy little chap, giving every impression of being well able to carry a man for a day on the hills. Slight feathering adds to his stature.

Elwyn Hartley Edwards in *Horse and Hound* (October 1990) states that though the feet and limbs are good, the neck is short, the shoulders straight and the back long. The Pottock has a straight profile, with a characteristic slight concavity between the eyes.

Today the National Pottock Association and the Direction des Haras are responsible for breed development, a far cry from pre-World War II days when this sturdy pony was a smuggler's pack animal. The long back bears that out.

The breed is sure-footed enough to have become a children's pony and a harness animal. It has also contributed to the French Riding Pony, in whose make-up are native French pony mares and Arab, Connemara, New Forest and Welsh stallions. The two other modern Pottock types are the Standard, of similar height to the Piebald, and the Double Pottock reaching up to 14.2 hands.

There are at least 35 different colours in Icelandic ponies, including several 'coloured'. The breed has its origin in the Norwegian horse, brought across by the Vikings around AD 1000. Though not indigenous, the breed has been kept pure from any outside influence for many centuries, and an Icelandic competing abroad at international shows cannot be taken home through disease risk. Most ponies master four gaits, including the 'tølt' (American 'rack'). This is a four-beat gait at trotting speed, very comfortable for the rider. The fifth gait is the pace.

Icelandic coloureds include red skewbald, bay skewbald and buckskin skewbald, with numerous piebalds and a combination of grey and white. Names bestowed on Icelandic ponies frequently reflect their colour combinations. In translation the lyrical Icelandic ring is regrettably lost, but in a list of names commonly given to Icelandics are twenty-four applying to coloured females, and twenty-six to coloured males, whether geldings or stallions. Blackhood, Horse-shoe, Girl in a Striped Dress, and Mantel are among them. Others describe such specific markings as White Cheek, Black Back, White Forehead or Jaw Mark. From the world of birds, Lapwing, Puffin and Oyster Catcher may well be imagined.

In the Icelandic pony, grey or dun predominate, while cream, dark brown, chestnut, palomino and black are also found. This breed is normally 12 to 13 hands, and is used on the country's sheep farms. Common practice in Iceland is to make hay on the enclosed fields during the long summer days, while the flocks fend for themselves on the mountain grazings, returning to their purpose-built houses in September. These September gatherings are the highlight of the farming year, impossible without sure-footed ponies. Icelandic farmers do not use the Border Collie so indispensable on British hills, but rather rely on their ponies to carry them and their provisions for days at a time when September brings summer's end to those northern latitudes. The ponies commonly winter out, growing long, shaggy coats, and surviving on hay left from the sheep sheds.

Skewbalds and spotteds are found in the Pinzgauer Noriker from Austria and Germany. Solid colours are more usual in this breed, said to have been bred under Roman rule in Noricum, a region approximating to modern Austria. Standing 16 to 16.2 hands, the Noriker is one of the few heavy breeds which has mountain associations.

Asia

Other breeds showing the same endurance and toughness as the Icelandic are the Kathiawari and the Marwari. Piebalds, skewbalds and creams appear among the chestnuts, bays, browns and greys of these two Indian breeds which are so alike that it is pointless to treat them separately. They share the characteristic ear tips which point in sharply when pricked, and almost touch.

Those two breeds are 14 to 15 hands, rather larger than the Kazakh from Kazakhstan in the USSR. Odd-colours and duns are found among its bays, chestnuts, greys and blacks. The Kazakh is as adaptable as a pony can be, surviving on snow or sand. It will produce over two gallons of milk a day, and may be fattened

An Indian pony described as a Mongolian type of 'country-bred' mare, and a useful troop
horse.

for meat. No wonder the seventh-century Kazakhstani nomads were buried with
their ponies, whose remains indicate that they were similar to today's.

The Americas

The Criollo has blue and white and red roan and blue roan among its more usual
solid colours. It is one of the world's hardiest breeds, and is the mount of the
gauchos who work the great stock ranges of South America. One of the best-known
horses of modern times is the Criollo skewbald Mancha (see pages 107–9).

The Falabella is a breed created by the family of that name in Argentina. It was
first imported into Britain in the late 1960s, where it is rare but spreading. The
breed is a miniature horse under 34 inches (as are all miniatures).

It has no breed standard regarding colour, and both spotted and parti-colours are

Valerie Underwood's Falabella mare Edwina.

encouraged. Breeders sensibly strive for a varied coat colour. 'The more interesting the coat, and the smaller the animal, the higher the price', they claim. In 1993 there were only some sixty pure-bred Falabellas in Britain, registered after a search into their breeding. Crosses have been made with Shetlands and Welsh Section 'A', but the offspring are not accepted in the registry. A Falabella, Valerie Underwood's high-stepping Edwina, tied for first place in 1992 at a leading Welsh show.

Between the introduction of the horse to North America and the settlement of range and prairie, a great many horses ran wild. Some had escaped from strings of saddle horses, some had been bred on the range. They were more properly called 'feral', and in 1934 J. Frank Dobie wrote a wonderfully lively book about them entitled *The Mustangs*.

He estimated that there were at one time a million mustangs in Texas alone, and a further million scattered throughout the American West. 'Halted in animated expectancy or running in abandoned freedom, the most spirited and inspiring creature ever to print foot on the grasslands of America', he wrote. 'Only by blotting out the present can one see those wild horses of the prairies. They have gone with the winds of vanished years. They carried away a life and a spirit that no pastoral prosperity could in coming times re-present.'

And some of them were parti-coloured – paints and pintos to the ranchers and cowboys (pinto from the Spanish word *pintado*, painted), piebalds and skewbalds to Britishers. Frank Dobie listed them:

> The wild ones – the coyote duns, the smokies, the blues, the blue roans, the snip-nosed pintos, the flea-bitten grays and the black-skinned whites, the shining blacks and the rusty browns, the red roans, the toasted sorrels and the stockinged bays . . . The splotched appaloosas and the cream-maned palominos, and all the others in shadings of colour as various as the hues that show and fade on the clouds at sunset – they are all gone now, gone as completely as the free grass they vivified.

If only there were some record of which foals ran with which mares, and details of the stallion of that particular *manada*, or group of mares! Such a record would have been impossible to tabulate, for observers had little more than galloping glimpses, and much work to do other than easing the task of future historians. Dobie stressed: 'The common idea that wild horses gradually degenerate through uncontrolled breeding is contrary to fact. Only the fittest stallions had chance to breed. Until the white man interfered, mustang stock did not degenerate any more than deer, antelopes, buffaloes and other wild species left to themselves degenerate.'

One trick of the mustangers was to send out a gentled stallion who would add wild horses to his bunch, enabling them to be corralled. Comanche was one such superior stallion, sent towards a *manada* of wild mares headed by a 'blooded jack', which contained two beautiful paint mules, both unbranded.

Comanche kicked and bit the mares' already scarred shoulders if they tried to escape, and eventually all but the jack were brought into a big pen. 'There were twenty-odd mares, eight or ten suckling colts, and an equal number of fillies, besides the two beautiful paint mules! Comanche was feasted.'

Other captures were less enduring. During the summer of 1882, three T-Anchor cowboys of the Texas Panhandle manoeuvred three mustangs – a black, a sorrel and a paint – into a gulch and roped them. After becoming fairly good cow horses they were turned loose with a big *remuda* in a quarter-million acre (390 square miles) pasture. The three mustangs bunched by themselves. Six hands took after them.

One reported later: 'We ran them for 15 miles, headed in one direction, south-east. They kept a quarter mile ahead of us. When they came to a fence, they went over it without touching a wire. That was the last any of us ever saw of those mustangs.'

Another 'coloured' had similar ideas. A tamed-down *manada* was walked around a big, strong cow pen on the plains for two days before being persuaded inside. But the stallion, a big pinto, cut off alone, was chased fifteen miles and then escaped.

In 1798 President Thomas Jefferson wrote requesting information on the wild horses of the West. A mustanger named Nolan had returned with a thousand horses, and promised one 'remarkable for colour' to Jefferson. Sadly, we can only guess that this was a paint. Nolan's mustanging was on the Grand Prairie of central Texas. Records show that he captured or bought 'duns, roans, grays, whites, blacks, sorrels, bays, browns and paints'.

A paint figured in one of the most memorable hunts undertaken by mustanger J. W. Moses, who wrote of his experiences in *Mustangs and Cow Horses* (1940) under the name of Sesom (Moses spelt backwards). A bright orange dun with white mane and tail, and a paint mule for which the owner offered a good reward, were followed by Moses and his friend Romaldo Longoria. After reaching the range they rode for three days before locating the pair. The ropers pitched camp, saddled fresh horses and waited for the mustangs to drink before starting after them. Don Romaldo cut off the paint mule and roped it, but Moses had a terrific chase after the dun, and his horse fell when just within roping distance. He was knocked unconscious, came to with a swollen knee, managed to mount and gave his horse his head. They arrived at a muddy hole, and then made for camp, where Don Romaldo had the paint mule securely tethered, and with his helper was about to start searching for Moses.

Let's end this account with an Indian story. A young man who travelled up the

Missouri in 1843 saw 'a beautiful Blackfoot pied mare carry, with hardly a touch of the reins, her rider on a three-mile chase after a dodging wolf. At the end, the motion of her nostrils was scarcely quicker than when she started.'

British breeds

Shire

Heavy cart horses were being bred in Britain during the eighteenth century, and by the early nineteenth were widespread on farms and in cities. Among there were piebalds and skewbalds, and two broken-coloured heavies were painted in 1810. The artist was J. C. Zeitter, the engraver J. Egan, and the picture's owner was

Pirate and Outlaw, draught horses painted in 1810 by J. C. Zeitter.

Andrew McCullen. The barrels depicted show that these were brewery horses, and it is to the brewing trade's credit that, almost two centuries later, brewers are still to the forefront with their heavy horse teams.

In 1810 the Shire was not officially so named. Its first five Stud Book volumes beginning in 1877 were entitled The English Cart-Horse Society, and not until 1886 was the name Shire officially adopted. Dray owners, grooms and the public all seem to have appreciated 'odd-coloured' heavies, but Shire breeders did not. Perhaps they were smarting from remarks by Hermann Biddell, author of that magnificent Volume 1 of the Suffolk Horse Society Stud Book 1880, which includes Suffolks of seven recognised shades of 'chesnut':

> The Shire-bred man is no wise particular. Watching the ring at the Royal, one sees black, brown, bay and chesnut; with or without white, whole-coloured or sandy roan. Breeders claim all shades as the 'true colours' of the Shire-bred proper.

Thus spake a Suffolk man! Yet there is nothing particularly clever about breeding chestnuts. Mate two together, and it is impossible to breed anything else!

In *The Shire Horse*, Keith Chivers records the spirited answer given by Sanders Spencer, pig breeder and controversial writer. Commissioned to report on the 1885 London Show (the Shires' main event), he wrote: 'I would class with Shire-breds the many-hued and coloured Shorthorn, and then ask him what two breeds of animal, and the crosses between them, are half as extensively bred all over the world, or can nearly approach them in usefulness or grandeur.'

Volume I of the English Cart-Horse Society Stud Book was retrospective, reaching back to Blaze 183, foaled in Leicestershire in 1770, and incidentally one of the 35 so named in that volume. No. 770 was Everett's Horse, a piebald foaled in 1825, and bred and owned by Everett of Broughton, Lincolnshire. He was sired by Holmes's Horse of Edwalton, with whom our trail ends.

We may conjecture whether Everett's Horse was ancestor to the parti-coloured Shires 'by no means uncommon in the Fen country', according to Sir Walter Gilbey in *Horses: Breeding to Colour* (1912). He instanced Mr B. B. Colvin of Hertford-shire, who in the mid-nineteenth century had a breed of piebald Shires on his Home Farm.

There appears to be a link between roans and parti-colours, and one roan stallion who made Shire history was The Old Strawberry, registered as England's Wonder

B. B. Colvin's plough teams of Shire horses in Essex, about 1844–55. His stud sadly lapsed on his death.

761. Foaled in Norfolk in 1861, he left his mark both there and in Montgomeryshire, where he was hired. Chivers tells us that he left roans of many hues, 'all with or without white legs and white patches, and even varieties of skewbald. In Montgomery and west Norfolk it was years before this tendency to oddity of colour died out.'

The Old Strawberry son Coming Wonder 3039 was a bay roan who travelled for many years in Wales, where he too left a vast number of strangely coloured progeny. By then breeders were tending to concentrate on solid colours. These they would register, but registering costs money, and the fact that skewbald and piebald Shires were not registered does not prove that they did not exist.

A skewbald Shire did its bit to cheer proceedings during those dark days when the heavy horse did indeed seem doomed to extinction. Chivers tells us:

> The depths were plumbed in 1955. Proceedings [at the Spring Show] opened in steady rain, carried across the ground by a cold wind. In the whole show, only 26 stallions, 28 mares and fillies and 14 geldings were forward. Then the weather improved, and a fine class of brood mares cheered everyone up. The next day, at S. T. Parker's auction, 64 horses were offered for sale and 42 sold. The top price was 60 guineas for a five-year-old mare – a skewbald!

That achievement could be repeated. Suppose one wanted to do something really spectacular, and breed a team of skewbald Shires as a real crowd puller? It is quite feasible. A tall, hairy and well-boned parti-coloured stallion could be found by asking down the travelling people's grapevine. Then he could be tested for homozygosity (see page 136) and if proven would breed parti-coloured offspring from solid-coloured Shire mares. At present such offspring could not be registered with the Shire Horse Society, but if demand for broken colours continues to grow at its present pace, Council might feel obliged to return to its roots and admit them.

Clydesdale

The breed standard of this Scottish heavy horse states: 'The colour should be preferably bay or brown, with a white stripe on the face, legs white over knees and hocks.' Enthusiastic secretary Robert Gilmour, Clydesdale Horse Society of Great Britain and Ireland, wrote in answer to my query: 'The Society does not recognise a Piebald or a Skewbald as a Clydesdale colour.'

Yet of all modern heavies, the Clydesdale shows unmistakable signs of overo markings. These may begin at the foot, and in some cases show unblemished white right up the hind leg, under the belly and way up the flank. Such animals are registered with the Society. In spite of the breed society's own rules, coloured horse people of the 1990s would say that a proportion of Clydesdales are undeniably overo. It takes us back to the vexed question of definition of piebald and skewbald, tobiano and overo.

While the Shire Horse Society bars roan or chestnut in stallions, the Clydesdales do not. They simply state a preference for bay or brown. The Clydesdale Horse Society information leaflet is indeed more informative than the standard. 'The colour is bay, brown or black, with much white on face and legs, often running into the body. It should be noted that chestnuts are rarely seen.' That last point has become outdated since Dr Christine Wallace Mann assembled a magnificent team of chestnut Clydes.

The Clydesdale Horse Society does not encourage roan, yet to many heavy horse people it is a typical Clydesdale colour. Northumbrian Mervyn Ramage drives a pair of blue roan Clydesdale geldings, Blue Print and Lenzie Jim, which delights the summer crowds. Horse people ignore their audiences at their peril! Another point is that roan Clydesdales are easily identifiable as such to the uninitiated,

A registered Clydesdale with pronounced colour pattern.

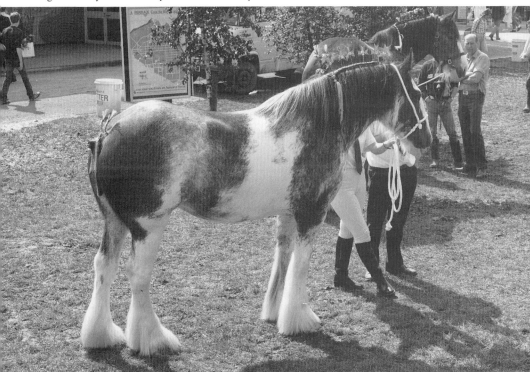

45

whereas only an expert can differentiate between some Shires and Clydesdales, and then be wrong!

Shetland pony

The Shetland Pony Breed Society was formed in 1890, and its first Stud Book was published a year later. The breed has spread to North America, Australia and Europe, and is the only British native pony society which still officially recognises parti-coloureds in its register. (Shetland Pony people tend to use the term 'coloured' for any non-black.)

Miss Eva Smith from Shetland has judged the breed at the Royal Highland Show. 'Having been brought up with coloured ponies, I have no difficulty in placing them against the solid colours, though I know that some people don't find it easy', she said. 'We often keep our black Shetlands on one area, and the coloureds on another part of the farm. This is to try and keep the blacks correct. We do put whole colours among the broken colours occasionally, but we don't always breed the colour we expect!'

Miss Smith pointed out that some early colour definitions are ambiguous. Prince of Howlland, foaled in 1881 and 41 inches high, is classed as piebald, yet described as red and white. Mares listed in Volume I include greys, browns, chestnuts, bays, piebalds and skewbalds, duns, blacks, dark browns and, significantly, blue-greys and whites. There is also a grey with a black strip down the back, a roan, a blue roan, a black with four white feet, a white and a cream with black legs. Dun and mouse are also found, while one skewbald was a stallion named Charlie.

With this variation in the foundation stock, it is easy to see how the present wide range in colours has occurred. The Shetland Pony Society and its modern members have certainly taken full advantage of such a variation to form an eye-catching showring line-up.

Yet leading breeder and exhibitor Robert W. R. Mackenzie in *The Standard Cyclopedia of Modern Agriculture* wrote, just before World War I: 'Pedigreed Shetland ponies can be got in almost any colour, but black and dark-brown are the most popular, and white markings are viewed with suspicion. A white hoof is seldom or never seen except in piebald ponies, and although these always command a market they are discouraged in the showring.'

In 1908, R. Brydon in de Trafford's *Horses of the British Empire* told us: 'The prevailing colour of the Shetland is black, not, however, a jet black, but what is known as Shetland black, a lighter and more slaty hue. Browns, bays, duns, chestnuts and piebalds are also common. The three latter colours, however, are not much in request, and by careful mating can be got rid of.'

Very probably piebald was discouraged by those breeding for the regular market of the Durham coal mines, where they were first introduced in 1847. Black or brown was obviously more suitable for such conditions, for which Brydon told us: 'A very short training suffices to accustom them to the change, and apparently they quickly become as contented and happy in the one position as the other [their native wilds].'

As Shetlands are no longer needed in the mines, those once valid reasons for favouring blacks and browns have passed also. Rather than trying to breed out piebalds, the little breed is today awash with beautiful parti-colours.

The 1990 Centenary Edition of the Shetland Pony Stud-Book Society magazine, a treasure for any horse lover, has 230 large, glossy pages packed with news and photographs of studs containing a high proportion of piebalds and skewbalds. Taken at random they include Doodle on her last appearance at Olympia before retiring. This little skewbald mare had regularly made the journey from the Shetland Isles with owner Mrs Helen Thompson, appearing at every performance of the Volvo Shetland Grand National since its inception. In the afternoons she went round all the charity boxes, meeting blind, deaf and dumb and cancer-suffering children, giving them much pleasure. Some had never met a pony and, sadly, might never do so again. In one hour Doodle raised over £1,000 for Esther Rantzen's Child Line Appeal. On a happier note, Prince William and Prince Harry came to say goodnight to her in her stable. A new mascot, Topsy, is taking over for this popular Volvo-sponsored event. She too was bred in Shetland, and is tiny and tri-coloured.

Kilcummer Stud on Bodmin breeds miniature Shetlands, starting at 28 inches. Sons and daughters of their senior stallion Fairy Flask (31 inches) include both piebalds and skewbalds. More skewbalds are found at Idolsfold House Farm, Kirdford, West Sussex. The bright bay stallion Hippominimus Huggy Bear (27½ inches) left a grand little filly out of the skewbald Ruskin Wendy, the foal being all white except for its head, upper neck and around the tail. At the Knock stud, Cumbria, the stallion Knock Good Luck has cleanly marked black and white, and ample bone.

On Shetland itself, Lochside ponies range from 28 to 40 inches, and from standard black through cream dun, silver dun, piebald, skewbald and chestnut to grey and golden dun. Another cleanly marked piebald is Seva Nice Fella (34 inches) from the Arosfa Deg Stud, which stresses temperament and colour. Ponies used by Broothom Riding and Trekking at Dunrossness, Shetland, include parti-coloureds tackling the heathery hills.

In a quite different environment, the skewbald Ringway became the Parachute Regiment's first Miniature Shetland mascot. He had a heated stable, luxurious transport, and a Pony Major in full-time care of the mascots. The 1st Battalion took Corporal Ringway to Berlin in 1974, and he was promoted to Sergeant Ringway after his steadiness on the Allied Forces and Queen's Birthday Parades in 1975. He died later that year in Berlin.

The immense popularity of piebald and skewbald Shetlands is shown by a glance through the 1990 Centenary Year sale reports. At Baltasound, Shetland, the skewbald filly foal Marie of Belmont realised 405 guineas against a filly average of £78, while the two-year-old piebald filly Pryde of Freefield sold for 460 guineas (£250 average). At the Reading sale, the piebald filly foal Merrivale Miss Ellie realised 1450 guineas, and the skewbald Parlington Chrissie 1325 guineas, against an average of 555 guineas. Seva Tomasina and Seva Tiddlywink, both piebalds, grossed 2700 guineas for Mrs M. Whitaker.

Why do not other breeds follow the Shetland's example and breed for this fascinating and rewarding range of colours? Horse and pony exhibitors must cater to the general public, often uninitiated and unable to distinguish between one solid coloured animal and another, but enthralled by the patterns on broken-coloured animals.

One of the finest trotting ponies ever known was a piebald Shetland. Beauty was owned by Richard Lacy, and in 1831 she trotted ten miles in 39½ minutes. This test was the subject of a wager, for Richard Lacy challenged all the world to produce a pony of equal size to beat her over the distance. None was forthcoming, so Beauty performed her remarkable feat without a pacer.

Several times she trotted a mile in 3 minutes 44 seconds. Then, on 3 August 1832, she began from the second milestone from Boroughbridge, North Yorkshire, and trotted seven miles out and seven miles back in 55 minutes 45 seconds. She did this with perfect ease, and 'but for the breaking of a rein would no doubt have accomplished 15 miles within the hour' according to a contempory report. Yet she stood less than 44 inches tall.

Beauty was imported from the Shetland Islands in 1824, and remained unbroken till six years old. An engraving in the possession of Lady Estelle Hope had been

Beauty, a fast trotting Shetland pony, the property of Richard Lacy.

'most respectfully inscribed by his obliged and obedient servant, R. Ackermann', acting for Mr Lacy.

Hackney

The early Hackney Stud Books are mines of information. In particular they list early examples of parti-coloured Hackneys of above-average performance. Parti-colours are still accepted today.

The piebald mare 228 Magpie (the mare's number precedes her name, the stallion's follows his) was foaled in 1870. Her sire was the black Confidence, her

A parti-coloured Hackney, still accepted for breed society registration today.

dam the skewbald 337 Spot, by Gant's Premier. Magpie was a great little winner both under saddle and in harness. She stood only 13.3½ hands high, so could compete in Under 14 and Under 14.2 hands classes. Volume I of the Hackney Stud Book devotes over half a page to her accomplishments.

'It is improbable that there has ever been so great a winner as Magpie, and possibly no more popular horse or mare has ever entered a show ring', wrote Vero Shaw in de Trafford's *Horses of the British Empire* (1908). 'She was bred in 1878 by Mr C. E. Cooke, of Litcham, Swaffham, Norfolk, and during her long career she won some four hundred first prizes, including ten successive victories at the Royal. In all cases where action was considered it was impossible to put her out of her place.'

Reasons for Magpie's excellence are not difficult to find. Her sire, Youngman's Confidence, was an unregistered horse, son of D'Oyley's Confidence, one of the five foundation sires of the modern Hackney.

'More than one strain of Hackney had a tendency to revert to pony size if bred too close', said breed authority Tom Ryder. 'Magpie is an instance of this. Her dam's sire, Gant's Premier, stood 15.2½ hands. Most Hackney ponies were evolved in this way and not through crossing with Dales or Welsh as some writers have it.'

Magpie was owned by William Pope of Downham Market, Norfolk. She was, said his daughter Miss Pope, 'a most pleasant ride'. In pairs and tandem she was frequently partnered by the brown Maritana, a 14 hands pony which won some £2000 in prize money for Mr Pope.

Magpie's skewbald dam Spot was foaled around 1864. She was by the non-registered Hackney Premier, and at this distance in time the parti-colour seems to have come only from the dam's side. Spot's dam was a skewbald by the Thorough-bred horse Mentmore, and her granddam a skewbald half-bred Arab.

Magpie's breeder Mr Cooke also bred 792 Movement from the skewbald Spot. That was in 1876, the sire being Washington 852 by the American trotter Shepherd F. Knapp. Movement, a skewbald, stood 14.3½ hands, and was owned by Henry Frisby of Buckingham Gate, London. Mr Frisby was a stockbroker, and one of the

Movement, pictured in 1888, and described as the 'winner of numerous prizes'.

first to own show harness horses as a hobby. High stepping hacks were in vogue at that time, and for the next 20 years or so, and Movement was shown up and down the country, both in harness and under saddle.

'She was a taller mare than Magpie, and not so good looking. She possessed more speed than her piebald half-sister, and her hock action was wonderful. But the little one beat her handsomely when they met at the Norfolk show, and the decision was generally endorsed', wrote Vero Shaw. He recalled the Crystal Palace Show of 1897, and 'Mr Mitchell's very showy, but rather too high-couraged, skewbald Marjorie'.

One of the largest-scale Hackney breeders was Cole Ambrose of Stuntney Hall, Ely, Cambridgeshire. He favoured piebalds and skewbalds, and he specialised in exports. Henry Walter Gath in the Argentine was a principle customer, who continued to breed parti-coloured horses there from the many he imported.

Stuntney Hall must have provided an endless feast of fascination and colour in those halcyon days before World War I, when roadsters were scarcely disputed. With horse transport at its zenith, Cole Ambrose set about providing a large number of stock roadsters. In the 1904 Stud Book he registered eight stallions and fifteen mares. These figures are somewhat misleading, as like many livestock breeders Mr Ambrose apparently found paperwork uncongenial, and seems to have registered his Hackneys when the mood struck him, which was not always every year.

A big Shire stud was also maintained. It is worth noting, however, that farming times were hard, and grooms and farm workers were paid only around £1 a week for very long hours.

Proof that the Hackneys alluded to were by no means exceptional in colour is given by Vero Shaw. He deplores the increase in chestnuts at the 1907 Hackney Horse Society show. 'Hence, no doubt, the increased value that attaches to brown and bay hackneys for harness purposes ... but for use in vehicles of a lesser size than landaus or state coaches there is, of course, a call for chestnuts, roans both red and blue, and also for skewbalds and greys, each of which possess their admirers.'

Fell

Today the Shetland is the only British native pony breed to accept parti-coloureds. Other breeds undoubtedly had them, including the Fell, New Forest and Welsh.

Modern registered Fell ponies must be black, brown, bay or grey. This is claimed to indicate their 'purity', yet early Stud Book entries show that parti-coloureds were once accepted.

Clive Richardson in *The Fell Pony* (1990) said: 'During the reign of Elizabeth I, skewbald as a colour was introduced into northern England and the Scottish borders by a new class of itinerant traders.' These 'tinkers' or 'potters' first had brown and white horses and later piebalds, and the two colours 'represented a sort of trademark, not unlike the Cistercian monks with their white horses', said Richardson. He continued:

> As the fancy colour was originally confined to the great war horses which were bred only by noblemen or at the royal studs ... the potters had to use their cunning to obtain the services of these inaccessible stallions. They did so by slipping their mares into the royal parks or breeding 'closes' where these stallions ran after nightfall, and reclaiming them before dawn.

Fell ponies were initially registered in 1898, in their own section of Volume V of the Riding and Polo Pony Society's stud book. 'Brough Hill ponies' was bracketed after their section title, to avoid confusion, that place being the site of the main autumn sale. Clive Richardson records:

> The following year the committee inspected and passed as being correct Fell type a piebald pony called The Mikado. Their indiscretion was due to the fact that they had met at The George Hotel in Penrith first and were quite drunk when they inspected the stallion. To camouflage their misdemeanour, they described the pony as black-brown with tan and white hind heels.

The Mikado claimed among his ancestors such redoubtable names as the Norfolk Trotters Marshland Shales, Old Grey Shales and Sportsman. Flying Childers, son of the Darley Arabian, also figured, so unsurprisingly The Mikado was a 'mile in under three minutes trotter'. His granddam could trot four miles in 11 minutes 29 seconds, won 17 successive trotting races and was only once beaten before being killed in her 36th year, Clive Richardson concluded.

That committee's conviviality may have given them extra courage, but I think they knew perfectly well what they were about. North country stockmen have a genius for combining business with pleasure without the latter affecting the former. The Fell is an ideal breed into which to re-introduce broken colours to its great advantage.

'The Mikado was not the only aberration in the early days of Fell pony registrations', said Clive Richardson. He cited other examples in the Fell register:

> a skewbald mare called Voreda who had been purchased at Brough Hill Fair and who won the Riding and Polo Pony Society medal at Penrith Show. There are other piebalds, a quarter-bred Arab ...The fifth Earl of Lonsdale ... owned a number of chestnut Fells, several having excessive white markings, and the Winders family of Caldbeck had a famous strain of roan ponies.

In 1912, a total of 217 mares were covered by six Premium Fell stallions. Though browns, bays, blacks and greys predominated, there were 13 chestnuts, five piebalds, one roan, one dun and one cream among the offspring.

Another amusing incident involving a parti-coloured Fell happened at Middleton-in-Teesdale in 1920. Two judges were split on the stallion class winner, one preferring the skewbald Sporting Times and the other the grey Hilton Fashion, so they called in a third man.

'The referee judge had been drinking in the local pub and was very much the worse for drink, but he staggered into the ring, swaying visibly,' said Richardson. 'Without even looking at the ponies he pointed with his stick and in a loud drunken voice shouted "Gee it to Baldie!" and that was that.'

The donkey

Averil Swinfen, author of the enchanting book, *The Irish Donkey* (1969), really fell for parti-coloureds in the 1960s. Grey asses were then common in Ireland, but Lady Swinfen chose blacks.

> We rested, happy with our lot, until a friend sent us a photograph of a skewbald or piebald donkey about to leave Dublin docks for England. We were fascinated by it and felt that one like it must be added to our number. Well, after many enquiries and advertisements in various newspapers for 'an unusual coloured donkey', we brought a pretty little skewbald filly of about nine months old. It was the fact of her price being so astonishingly in excess of the price paid for one-colour donkeys, combined with the intense interest we had as to how they bred, that really decided us to have a Stud Farm.
>
> After that everything snowballed: more land, more donkey mares and fillies

and, perhaps the most important ingredient of a stud farm, some handsome and well-bred stallions, until we reached our present strength of between 50 and 60 animals (not including the visiting mares) and about 40 acres of land, plus more held under lease.

We have four different coloured stallions at service. A white, a piebald and a skewbald standing here with a black one on lease nearby. A handsome chestnut colt will soon join them, all bred in Ireland.

Lady Swinfen posed the question of how piebalds and skewbalds arrived in the donkey world. The colours were not seen in Ireland until the mid-twentieth century, and she believes that white is the primary colour in the breeding of both skewbalds and piebalds. 'I wonder could it be that only in recent years have African and Asiatic asses ceased to meet as wayfarers and have settled down long enough to produce over the generations broken-coloured progeny?'

Broken-coloured animals, including horses and cattle, around parts of the west of Ireland are, as we have seen, referred to as 'batty'. 'When our first broken-coloured donkeys arrived', said Averil Swinfen, 'the locals asked to see the "batty asses".' Her researches took her to the word 'Battak' as the name of a Sumatra pony in 1905. 'According to this book these ponies were bred in the Battak range of hills in Sumatra, and were a regular export to Singapore, being on an average 11.3 hands high and of many colours, with piebalds and skewbalds in the majority.'

The original colour of the unimproved Battak pony is said to have been mouse-grey, with a black stripe down the back. Arab blood was introduced for cross-breeding because all neighbouring and local princes, sultans and chieftains coveted the pure white, red-eyed (albino) ponies, without any markings, combining 'the fire and beauty of the Son of the Desert with the hardiness and endurance of the Battak pony'.

It seems that Arab horses, with their range of white, grey, bay, chestnut, brown or black, produced piebalds, skewbalds and roans when mated to the mousey-grey Battaks, as well as introducing their own colouring. The white, being so greatly prized, was probably crossed with a whole range of other colours in an attempt to breed that valuable hue, and broken colours were as a result often thrown up. Economics were ever a major force in livestock changes.

Lady Swinfen states: 'In the ancestry of any broken-coloured asses that I have knowledge qf, there has always been a white parent or ancestor, and the more

A parti-coloured mule, Helen Clements' Muffin, at a Somerset wedding.

white forebears in the lineage, the more likelihood of getting broken colours.' The intervention of any other colour just added to the mixture. Yellowish patches sometimes appeared on the onager or wild Asiatic ass, and the same yellowish colour appears in many broken-coloured asses today.

The first broken-coloured donkey that Averil Swinfen saw in Ireland was in Adare, County Limerick. 'He was bought from a well-known circus by the late Earl of Dunraven in 1950 for £40, then a very high price for a donkey. He is a beautifully marked gelding called Mr Buttons and is companion to many of the horses in their stud.'

The hooves seem to be the first part of the animal to show signs of colour changes. Averil Swinfen noticed that broken-coloured donkeys have had either broken-coloured hooves, white hooves or a mixture of each, and never four black ones. 'An ordinary coloured, mouse-grey foal born to us this season by a skewbald sire out of a mid-brown mare has got all hooves broken-coloured.'

5 The gypsy type of coloured horse

'Gypsy gold does not chink and glitter. It gleams in the sun and neighs in the dark.'
Saying of the Claddagh Gypsies of Galway

The British Isles recognise nine native breeds of pony. They are the Dales, Fell, Highland, Shetland, Exmoor, Dartmoor, New Forest, Connemara and Welsh.

Perhaps we should consider as a tenth the gypsies' coloured roadster. 'Breed' is defined in the Shorter Oxford English Dictionary as 'Race, stock, strain; a line of descendants perpetuating particular hereditary qualities.' Though the gypsy animal sometimes exceeds the accepted pony height of 14.2 hands, so do some of the larger recognised breeds in these days of improved upland grazings.

However, gypsy horses and ponies have no breed society and no stud book. This does not mean that ancestry is unknown; far from it. I am frequently impressed by the detailed knowledge of back-breeding which is displayed.

Ivan Armitage, who lives in a 'settled' caravan at Spaldington, East Yorkshire, said that every outstanding gypsy stallion would be known about by all the travelling people within two years. There is of course no outside means of authenticating these claims, but we can all point to examples of written pedigrees that are dubious in the extreme. I have great faith in the memory, knowledge and accuracy of the genuine gypsy horseman.

Ivan Armitage, who cannot read or write, and his friend Alan Harwood elucidated the following points of the gypsy roadster when my wife and I joined them one hard-freezing January night. We all sat outdoors on wooden boxes around a blazing wood fire, which not only kept us warm but afforded sufficient light to take notes. We drank tea from Crown Derby mugs handed round by the gypsy children. I've learnt much less from many a highly organised seminar in sumptuous surroundings.

The unwritten 'breed standard' is for a horse or pony 14, 14.1 or 14.2 hands high. If much bigger it costs more to feed, shoe and harness. It is a 'road' horse as opposed to a 'land' horse. Its purpose is to walk smartly along the level or uphill road, and break into a trot where going and gradient allow.

A nice, small head is sought. It should not be coarse in any way, but in proportion to the rest of the body. Ears should be fairly large; they enable the horse to hear the driver better on the road, and some believe they indicate a quieter

The traditional gypsy vanner.

animal. This hearing ability has never been more important than when driving amongst today's fast traffic. Watch a gypsy horse on the road, and its ears will be twitching all the time.

The normal eye colour is brown, but a wall eye is regarded as little detriment. When the blinkers are on, it is hardly noticed. Wall or odd-coloured eyes certainly occur more among piebalds and skewbalds than among solid-coloureds. The face is seldom Roman-nosed, and may be slightly concave. The forelock is long; it is in itself a form of protection, and is associated with a long mane and tail.

The neck should be short and strong, and the shoulder straight. We are dealing with a driving horse and, though most gypsy horses are ridden at times, they are bred primarily to do the job of covering long distances economically while drawing loads of up to a ton. The back may therefore be too broad for a comfortable ride.

The animal should be short-coupled and deep-bodied. Forearms should be strong, knees large and flat, and the cannon short and strong. A springing pastern and a well set-up heel are desired. A broad and round foot is essential, preferably black. However, few coloured horses have black feet. They are more usually striped or white, but a poor foot on a gypsy horse is seldom found. Regular performance testing ensures that those unable to withstand the hard roads soon find a fresh home.

Hindquarters should be strong and powerful: 'apple-cheeked' is the roadman's apt description. The tail should be set at moderate height, not as high as an Arab's, but higher than a carthorse's. The tail is a vital appendage. Tails on some of these gypsy horses have to be seen to be believed; not only are they long enough to sweep the ground, but the width and density are incredible. When the owner of a 'full tail' turns its back to the wind, it is sheltered by the equivalent of half an overcoat. Add to that the thick coat, and it becomes apparent why such an animal can thrive in an open field in mid-winter with only a little hay, when thin-skinned, light, 'kipper-ribbed' types would starve to death. If the tail becomes too long, it is shortened by downward knife sweeps, never by trimming across with scissors.

The gypsy 'coloured cob' has no precise standard for its markings. Alan Harwood likes two-thirds white to one-third colour. Ivan Armitage seeks a fifty-fifty proportion. A very few people seek an almost all-white animal with just an odd

A 'full tail' and ample feather on a gypsy cob.

Mane, tail and feather in abundance.

Coloured cobs are retained even in urban surroundings.

patch of colour, or one with very little white. These colours are no mere fad. It is vital to be able to see the lead horse on a dark or foggy night; for that reason, the off-leader in a four-horse team was often either grey, piebald or skewbald.

Another advantage is that the coloured horse carries its own identification. Stealing was more common fifty or sixty years ago, when city dealers might raid country fields. A plain-coloured horse could easily be lost among a penful of similar ones, but a coloured animal stood out and, furthermore, could be positively identified by those who had sat behind it hour after hour. With the present rise in horse values, thieving is again on the increase, and a parti-coloured animal is still a slight detriment to the thief. That does not mean that freeze-branding is unnecessary, but it stands out remarkably clearly on a piebald or skewbald (see illustration page 94).

It is a picturesque notion to think that the coloured cob accompanied the gypsy's ancestors centuries ago from the Middle East. There is little evidence to support such a view. The English gypsy caravan started after the Industrial Revolution, and though no statistics are available, there were probably few caravans as we know them before about 1880.

Anthony Dent in *Donkey: The Story of the Ass from East to West*, claims:

> The donkey was probably brought into Devon and Cornwall by the gypsies, who had long been keeping it on the dry heaths of Norfolk. Certainly when the Romanies first arrived in the New Forest they had not two horses to rub together, and all the earliest English pictures of gypsies show them carrying all their goods on pack-asses, without wagons, and living entirely in benders.

Brian Vesey Fitzgerald in *Gypsies of Britain* (1944) writes: 'There cannot be the slightest doubt that tents and ponies, not living waggons and teams of piebalds, are the true possessions of the Gypsies.'

Even when caravans first arrived, they were not necessarily drawn by coloured horses. The gypsies of the time were very poor, and could afford only such horses as other people did not want. 'We learnt how to cure "dodges", and to use a horse with a "dodge"', said Ivan Armitage, whose grandfather arrived penniless from Romania after World War I. Romania is where the term Romany originated.

These unwanted horses certainly contained a proportion of parti-coloureds. Most devotees of whole-coloured breeds were horrified if their strain threw up a piebald or skewbald. It happened, among Thoroughbreds, Arabs and others, and the innocent offender was either put down or sold somewhere other than the local market.

Around the World War II period, gypsies had a fashion for spotted horses. This did not last; perhaps the difficulties of breeding true were too great. In any case the parti-coloureds took over, augmented in the post-1945 slump of most horse breeds by piebalds and skewbalds bought to save them from the butcher. Gypsies, along with only a few individuals and companies, deserve our gratitude for keeping a nucleus of harness and heavy horse lines when cheap mechanisation seemed set for a complete take-over.

Despite its varied ancestry, the modern gypsy pony is fairly well fixed in type. Though the Hackney was one breed tried in the early days, apparently it did not 'nick'. The ideal type then, as now, was the thick, strong Dales pony, active yet a great puller. If a nicely marked coloured one of the sort appeared, it was kept. If it was a bad colour, it was sold. In the 1950s, parti-coloured horses rose in value and became status symbols to the travelling people. One red and white Shire foal was bought by them, and eventually sold as a drum horse. Another gypsy bought two parti-coloured Thoroughbreds which the owner couldn't get rid of fast enough!

During this time, temperament became all-important. The buyer who could 'master anything on four legs' had vanished. The new horse owners had no desire to spend time and risk life and limb trying to tame a wrong 'un. Besides, the gypsies' horses were almost as much part of the family as were their numerous children, and an unreliable temper could not be tolerated. So the parti-coloured horses generally are of placid temperament.

'The temperament of these coloured horses depends on how they are bred', stressed John Shaw, a carriage painter from Milnrow, Rochdale, Lancashire. 'They are generally docile, harking back to the carthorse temperament, but of course some of the halfbred trotter types have more mettle.' He bears out the comparatively recent emergence of the coloured horse as a gypsy animal. 'These gypsy horses started in the 1950s through crossing Dales and Fell pony mares with Clydesdale stallions', said John Shaw. 'The stallions used were often roan with a lot of white, giving rise to a variety of colours. You don't see so many entires of that type now.'

There were more Dales with white legs in the 1950s, possibly through earlier crossing with Clydesdales in an attempt to breed a heavier animal for ever-bigger farm machinery, most of which was designed for lowland conditions. The cross was not regarded as a success by Dales pony people, but it undoubtedly happened.

63

While in the 1950s the gypsies would use anything they could get hold of, they are now more particular, said John Shaw, who keeps horses of his own. 'Very big, hairy coloureds are now in vogue. They are status symbols, owned by someone who wants something to look at, but they are not really an economical animal. They cost too much to feed, harness and shoe, and though they have good, big feet, they don't stand up to the work. For that you want the vanner type of 14.3 to 15 hands.'

The current vogue for hairiness below the knee is not without danger. Shire breeders around the turn of the century worshipped hair, to the extent that one of their most successful, James Forshaw, said: 'Give me the hair and I will make a leg.' The fashion eventually rebounded, as hairy monsters caused so much stable work and were subject to 'grease' and other leg troubles. In Australasia, North America and South Africa, where teams were large and labour scarce, the hairy legs were laughed to scorn, and the clean-legged Percherons, Suffolks and Belgians predominated.

Besides the big, hairy beasts, another trend in parti-coloureds is towards the trotter with plenty of action. 'To breed these, a Welsh Section D is often used. He keeps the feather and he keeps the bone, and he has a smart action without being too extravagant,' John Shaw told me. 'Why not a Hackney?' I asked. 'Because the modern Hackney tends to be much lighter in bone than the Welsh. Where do you find a good, big Hackney horse? The tendency is towards Hackney ponies for the showring. Undoubtedly there are some strong Hackney stallions with sufficient bone, but coloured horse breeding tends to be a local affair. Travelling people don't go far afield for entires if they can find something suitable nearer home.'

Though the Hackney was used to bring action to the Welsh Cob, it is so long ago that it has merged with the cob characteristics, and that is what the travelling people want. Welsh Section C (Welsh pony of cob type) is also favoured, as out of the larger mares the Section D stallion might leave foals that will grow bigger than the favoured vanner type.

John Shaw owned a Shire cross Welsh Section D stallion, black, 15 hands and of vanner type who went like a Hackney. His foals were different from the 'classy ones at classy prices' in vogue today. 'The colours tended to come from the female', he said. 'Welsh Section D people seem to like their chestnuts and blacks.'

He recalled a 15 hands strawberry roan horse which was put to 13.2 and 13.3 hands coloured mares. 'The foals were generally coloured, though I recall one roan with white legs', said John Shaw.

One stallion was white with very pale blue roan patches. He was supposed to be a full-bred Clydesdale, and his foals were all either bays or blacks. Another good stallion that John Shaw owned stood 15.2 hands. He was by a Clydesdale out of a Welsh Section D mare, and was white with black patches. A powerful, feathery horse, he was a bit clumsy, and was sold to draw a landau at Blackpool.

The performances of some of the parti-coloured gypsy cobs are now legendary. One was introduced to a milk round as a two-year-old, and continued in daily service for 26 years with never a day off. Not until the round was sold and the new owner logged the distance in his van was it discovered that that mare had covered 75 miles every day. The work was light, and she was fit and well fed. She then bred seven foals, not starting her maternal career until she was 28 years old.

Another left the Vale of York for Brough Hill, near Appleby, Cumbria, at 4 a.m., hauling only her medium-weight driver on an empty dray. The distance was 105 miles, and taking her own speed and having several rests, she arrived at 4 p.m. Immediately a man approached. 'I've passed you three times on the way. How much is she?' The price was asked and given on the spot. The mare had conquered the long if mainly gradual uphill haul from Scotch Corner to a high point of the Pennines at an average 8¾ m.p.h.

Appleby Fair

Anyone with a passion for broken-coloured horses should visit Appleby Fair. Staged in early June during the week following the Derby, it is a true Mecca for horse lovers. Spend a few days there, and you may well leave with the feeling that there is little worth doing in this life other than breeding, rearing and training parti-coloured horses.

Appleby is a Cumbrian market town just off the A66, and its New Fair is staged on rising ground outside. The aptly named Fair Hill is reserved for gypsies' caravans, and comprises an elevated group of fields surrounded by higher hills. The North Pennines stretch to the east, while westwards the Lakeland fells are etched in blue-black outline.

Against this magnificent backcloth the gypsies and travelling people muster each year, as they have since 1685 under the protection of a charter granted by King James II. They bring with them their coloured mares, yearlings, and others that they may have picked up during the preceding twelve months. The latest foal crop is there for inspection, and the stallions that sired the youngsters will probably be grazing nearby. These foals are handled from birth by the many children in the

In surroundings far from a tidy dealer's yard, these Appleby Fair horses (*above and below*) await buyers.

The asking price was high for this thick-set mare, heavily in foal to a coloured stallion. The clear division between colour and white in the magnificent mane is a definite selling point.

camps. They are haltered at a few days old, and soon learn to walk alongside their dams hitched to a moving caravan. By their first birthday they are half-broken; by their second they have learnt to accept saddle, bridle and collar.

Gypsy horses have no precise breaking period. All they learn is instilled naturally, absorbed during daily routine. They are ridden by wiry boys whose featherweight frames do no harm to equine spines. They walk for miles through buzzing traffic. They are fitted with jangling harness, to which traces are added sooner or later as the most natural thing in the world.

Word regarding the horses' ancestry may be relied on at least as much as that of their counterparts in settled life. Perhaps that is not much recommendation! 'Horsemen live by what they say', one dealer told me, and because a pony is said to be 14.1 hands high, that does not necessarily mean that he is 14.1 hands! As Miss

The author (*right*) admires a trotting horse.

Cecilia Shute observed in Somerville & Ross's timeless *Some Experiences of an Irish RM*: 'No one will ever explain to me why horse-coping is more respectable than cheating at cards . . . there is no forgiveness for dealing yourself the right card, and no condemnation for dealing your neighbour a very wrong horse!'

The Fair offers unrivalled opportunities simply to get your eye in, to absorb the vast range of types and colours available. I wrote in *Horse World Annual* 1970:

> Horsemen and women gravitate there, drawn by some power as intangible as the magic of a stable. Much hand slapping accompanies each deal, both parties seeking the final and binding handshake at their own valuation.
>
> Long lines of horses are tied up under the hawthorn hedges or to a handy caravan. There is no rota of sale, and so you must ask the owner – when he can

Blue-roan and white is a popular colour at Appleby. Like most of the horses there, this stallion is traffic proof.

'Out of the river at Appleby'. Oil on canvas by Malcolm Coward.

be found – to show an animal that interests you – when there is room on the track, and Mad Harry and his trotting horse are at a safe distance.

You may hear of horses with every equine virtue and the prospect of eternal life here on earth, of faultless breeding and hardy rearing. They will be extolled by silver-tongued orators who might have come direct from a nineteenth-century parliament. But, unless you really are one yourself, take an expert with you.

Yet there is much to be learnt here even though you have no intention of writing a cheque, or rather of parting with wads of £10 and £20 notes which are the only acceptable currency. You will find cobby piebald stallions with incredibly wavy feather and mane, the status symbols of the 1990s.

Among the most valuable broken colours are the trotting horses. One in 1992 was rumoured to be on offer at 'three and a half', whispered with the air of one bestowing a significant favour by accepting £3,500 for such a steed. A tiny piebald

Shetland with cart to match attracted throngs of admirers, while a pair of skewbald mules were never without viewers. But for the serious student, the different markings and proportion of colour to white are fascinating.

Dun and white seems to be a selling colour. Chestnut and white runs it close, as does grey or blue-roan and white. Some horses had missed the black paint brush apart from a few head markings, including circles round the eyes, and a small patch on the rump.

There is opportunity to note eye colour. Pale blue eyes are associated with much white, and may be picked on as a weak point by the potential buyer, even though there is no proof that they are a character indicator. Though you yourself may like them, your eventual customer may not. It is always a sound rule not to give more for an animal than you could reasonably expect in the case of a forced, sudden sale.

The Fair now has three long rows of trade stands, when a few years ago there was nothing but some harness piled outside vans. These stands are an indicator of the broken coloured horse's popularity. Tea towels with gypsy caravans and piebalds and skewbalds abound. Artists depict the broken colours against a mountain setting or a stream, while plates, pots and mugs are adorned with prettily marked animals. Slate table mats glisten with black or brown and white ponies, with tea trays printed with similar scenes. Books of old photographs of the Fair are a mine of information about types and colours in days gone by.

6 The breed societies

The USA

In North America, associations for coloured horses are divided into Paints and Pintos. It was not always so. The Paint was derived from the Pinto, and the organisational split came around the mid-twentieth century.

Early horses died out in America, for reasons unknown, to re-appear with the Spanish Conquistadores under Cortez in 1519. Colonial Spain then developed its ranches, and stocked them well with horses. Marauding Indians stole some of these, and others escaped to run free and breed among themselves. Their offspring formed the nucleus of the mustang herds (see pages 38–41) that spread across the Great Plains and provided a reservoir of horses for Indian braves.

By the early nineteenth century there were thousands of wild (or more correctly, feral) horses in the West. Travellers of the period reported numbers of piebalds or skewbalds among them. It is not known how many. The coloured horse stands out in a crowd, and would be prominent among the ruck of bays, blacks, browns and greys. All these horses changed the Plains Indians' way of life. From primitive farmers and gatherers of wild fruits they became nomadic horsemen, both warriors and huntsmen.

Comanche Indians were claimed by contemporary historians to be the finest horsemen on the Plains, and they favoured parti-coloureds for a strikingly simple reason; their steeds were already bedecked with war paint! Coloured horses have been found painted on buffalo robes, proof if it were needed of the Comanches' affection for them. The Longhorn trail from Texas to the railheads in Kansas and Missouri brought the singing cowboy into his own, and among his favourite songs were 'Goodbye Old Paint, I'm leaving my home' and 'I ride Old Paint and I lead Old Dan'.

Deming, Forney, Remington, Russell and Seltzer were artists of the time who depicted the coloured horse in its Old West setting. By the beginning of the twentieth century, more Indians had been forced onto reservations, and cowboys were becoming mechanised, a continuing trend that led to a reduction in the number of parti-coloureds with the general decline in working horses.

America, cradle of the internal combustion engine, was also first to spearhead the horse's revival. In the 1950s, heavy and light horse breeding began to expand, more than a decade in front of a similar UK trend. The Pinto Horse Association of America was incorporated in 1956 in California. Its aim was to keep accurate records and to further the Pinto through selective breeding. It expanded from small beginnings, and is now based in Fort Worth, Texas. Pinto ponies were registered separately, and the horses were divided into 'types': stock, pleasure, saddle and hunter.

At the same time another group was quietly developing breeding programmes and promoting a registry for the American Paint Horse. Initially, the Paint was developed as a stock horse type. Its conformation was suitable for a wide range of abilities, while retaining the colour markings. A racing type has also been developed.

Bloodlines of American Paints come from Paints, Thoroughbreds and Quarter Horses only. Animals showing the characteristics or distinguishing qualities of any other breed, including draught breeds and ponies, are not accepted for registration with the American Paint Horse Association (APHA). However, the APHA retains the right to register any horse that is outstanding in conformation and performance even if it lacks the proper documentation to prove the bloodline requirement. But if its bloodlines or characteristics are other than from the accepted sources, it will not be registered.

Each Paint is unique in colour pattern. The range runs from almost total colour to almost total white with minimal dark markings. The darker colours range from very light to almost black, and encompass all the hues known in the horse world. It will not harm to refer again to the guidelines regarding colour pattern (pages 26–33), distinguishing between overo and tobiano.

There were two Paint registries in the early 1960s, the American Paint Stock Horse Association (APSHA) and the American Paint Quarter Horse Association (APQHA). From the showing and utility viewpoints there was little difference between the two, and in 1965 they united to form the American Paint Horse Association (APHA).

One result of the amalgamation was a further rapid rise in registrations. By January 1970, over 14,000 Paints had been registered from all fifty American States, Canada, Mexico and Central America. This compared with 250 registered horses in the first year, and today the Association is the sixth largest in the USA.

The first Stud Book published in 1966 contains colour photographs and statistics on over 3,000 Paints. The Association gave early encouragement to Paint owners to enter Open classes, and the first Paint to reach the Top Ten in the International Cutting Award was offered a substantial purse.

In 1968, 97 Paint shows were held, with 7,492 entries. In the following year, 119 approved shows attracted over 7,500 entries. Team roping, calf roping, flat racing and cutting were among the activities of those early days.

Today, over 80 affiliated American Paint Horse clubs promote activities on a regional, state, national and international level. APHA has affiliated clubs in Canada, Germany, Mexico, Australia and Italy, and other countries are showing positive interest. Records are kept of members' showing and racing activities. Outstanding show, contest and race Paints are recognised through various award programmes including the Register of Merit, Superior Horse, APHA Champion and APHA Supreme Champion.

During the last 25 years, the Paint has taken its rightful place as one of the world's most popular horse breeds. Its versatility is demonstrated to public and horse breeders alike. 'American Paints are equine athletes with a distinctively different coat pattern that sets them apart from all others', says APHA.

Don Chambers, manager of Louella's Thirsk stud, with Sonny Steele, chestnut overo of the stock horse type, with much Quarter Horse breeding in his pedigree.

Another American Paint Horse owned by the Louella Stud, D Bar S Blue Bayou, a black overo with a Quarter Horse dam.

The Association has two membership categories – annual and life. Regular members receive reduced rates for registering horses, besides voting rights and office or committee privileges. There is access to a wide range of Paint products, services and programmes, a quarterly newsletter and the Paint Horse Journal. The APHA hosts both a National Championship and a National Youth World Show each summer. These shows encourage families to compete in youth, amateur and open competitions, all under one roof at different times during the week. An annual major sale sponsored by the APHA is vital to the horse calendar.

Apart from showring competition there is competitive trail riding, chariot racing, cattle roping and team penning, and play days. Rodeo and endurance riding takes place in every state during the year. There is also plenty of scope for non-competitive horsemanship with afternoon rides, weekend trail rides, and parades.

75

The American Paint Horse is now claimed to be an economical animal with colour and spirit, yet possessing gentleness and good sense. A quarter of a century's breeding to develop its best qualities as a stock type horse are augmented by its singular colour pattern.

One of the interesting departments of the American Paint Horse Association is the Youth Development Foundation. Not only does it encourage better horsemanship, but it provides resources for young students in veterinary medicine, journalism, business, law, computer science, or agriculture. Scholarships are provided for students of the new equine technology. The Foundation is under no illusions about the complexities of Paint genetics, and research to determine the genetic cause of white foal syndrome and Paint patterns is useful in the study of other genetic diseases of the horse. 'The issues of tobiano/overo horses are so specific and complicated that researchers cannot work to unravel the genetic mysteries without funding from specific sources', says the Foundation.

Another APHA department is the racing department, which controls Paint Horse racing on tracks throughout the western USA. Horse and harness racing were both well established in North America when the Paints were becoming organised in the mid-twentieth century. So Paint racing had a slow start; the colourful Paint had to prove itself on bush tracks against the great Quarter Horses of the late 1940s. Those that succeeded included Little Nip and Painted Joe, two horses that set the standard for today's Paints bred from winning Thoroughbred and Quarter Horse bloodlines.

Britain

Coloured Horse and Pony Society

In September 1983 the Coloured Horse and Pony Society (CHAPS) was inaugurated in Britain. One of its chief aims was to combat prejudices that undoubtedly reacted against parti-coloured animals in mixed classes. A decade later, these colours are now more acceptable, and the two British societies can both take some credit. In fact, broken colours are now on the verge of becoming fashionable, but we shall always owe a debt to those who fought for them in the first place.

CHAPS encouraged county show organisers to establish classes for parti-colours. Through its Performance Award Scheme and provision of rosettes and prize money it offered practical assistance. Such classes have become very popular, and other shows are following the Cheshire County's lead to their own and the parti-coloured horse's advantage.

An excellent start was made when Sir John Miller GCVO, DSO, MC, became the first Patron of CHAPS. He was then the Queen's Equerry, and the Society was greatly helped when Her Majesty loaned two of her coloured stallions to stand at stud at accessible stables. Michael Simons MRCVS became Vice President, to be joined by Mr Douglas Bunn, Master of Hickstead. Miss Penelope Shephard was the first secretary.

An unsettled period followed, but CHAPS has now overcome its difficulties and has embarked on constructive schemes which include a stud book of registered stallions, mares and young stock and an annual stallion directory. Four regional shows now culminate in a National Championship, and the Society is affiliated to 70 other shows.

In 1993, CHAPS registered 57 stallions to veterinary standards, based on those in use by the Hunter Improvement Society, and is affiliated to the National Stallion Association. Membership approached one thousand.

In his capacity as CHAPS Stud Book Manager, Ivan Mears has received interesting observations from members. They had often owned a 'coloured' as a child, invariably with pleasant memories. Another category had always liked the piebalds and skewbalds, but until recently had been apprehensive about admitting their preference.

Guidelines are offered by CHAPS for classifications for Show Pony, Working Hunter Pony, Working Hunter Horse, Hunter Horse/Pony, Riding Horse/Pony, and Hack. In these classes, manes are to be plaited and tails plaited or pulled. Tack is to be simple snaffle or double or Pelham, with a martingale allowed in Working Hunter classes, when all competitors must jump.

Cobs are classed as 13 to 15.1 hands high, to be shown natural with full manes, tails and feathering (if any). If hogged, feathering must be removed, and tails pulled or plaited.

All Native 'types' (e.g. Welsh type, Shetland type, Mountain and Moorland type) must be shown in their natural state. Pulling of manes or tails is barred, as are trimmed heels or whiskers.

In the CHAPS regulations, Skewbald, Piebald, Tricolour, Tobiano and Overo must have a pied patch four inches above the level of stifle and elbow. A straight line is taken between the two, and any pied markings below this cannot be classed as tobiano or overo.

Two CHAPS licensed stallions: (*above*) D'Artagnon, an Irish-bred stallion, shows his ability competing under side saddle; (*opposite page*) Top Tiger by Hill Farmer TB, winner of the Working Hunter Championships at the CHAPS show in 1992.

The CHAPS definitions are:

TOBIANO – Upper Pied – White area along and down topline.
OVERO – Lower Pied – White area coming from belly – bottomline.

Manes and tails may also be pied, or have pied in them (this excludes greys or palominos) to be classified as a Coloured. The Coloured Horse and Pony Society of Great Britain staged a two-day show at the Three Counties Showground, Malvern, Worcestershire, in mid-July 1991. The show was affiliated to Ponies Association (UK), the Side Saddle Association and the Western Horseman's Association.

Classes included Best Turnout (Ridden), split into those kept at grass for at least ten months of the year and those stabled. There were five classes of jumping from Novice to Open, followed by Working Hunter Ponies in four classes. Working Cobs and Small and Large Working Hunters had their own classes and championship. In Dressage and Equitation, particular attention was paid to manners and way of going. The Western Trail is a thoroughly practical class, involving opening,

Soulbury Island God, shown successfully as a yearling at both CHAPS and non-coloured shows.

passing through and closing a gate without dismounting; walking over four spaced logs; then backing between two poles. Riders next had to remove and replace post from a mail box, sidepass to left and right over a single pole, and turn around in a six foot square. Driving, Best Weight Carrier and Best Rider concluded the first day.

The second day began with riding, including side saddle, Best Conditioned horse, and Western Pleasure under Western tack. The all-important Leading Rein Pony class was followed by Veterans In-Hand, and by breed classes for geldings, brood mares and foals, stallions and youngstock. The stallion produce groups provided a fitting finale.

British Skewbald and Piebald Association

The British Skewbald and Piebald Association was inaugurated in 1989. This Society's objects are to further interest and pleasure in skewbalds and piebalds, to improve their status and help members maximise their horses' potential. Equine welfare and charities are to be supported, and responsible breeding encouraged. Membership is open to all persons with an interest in skewbald and piebald horses and ponies.

A register has been instituted, open to any skewbald or piebald horse or pony. Its advantages are:

(a) To give the horse/pony an identity with a recognised registration document showing his/her photographs and details;

(b) To record changes of ownership;

(c) To be an official document for any future breeding plans.

Many good coloureds are of unknown breeding, but that does not bar them from registration. Nor does registration with another society. Two identical side-on photographs are required. Details required include colour, sex, date of birth (if known), adult height, and freeze brand or any other brand marks. Any known ancestry and current registration is added if available.

The Association offers a free BSPA rosette to show secretaries to award in their coloured horse or pony class. The winner need not be a BSPA member, and no affiliation to the Association is required. Apparently some Show Secretaries have asked that entries be restricted to members only, for fear that the local gypsies would turn up with all their ponies, 'some of which may not be in the best of health'! This seems an extraordinary attitude. Most gypsies are not interested in

A skewbald and a piebald – Irish-bred cobs ready for the show ring.

conventional showing, and through their 'survival of the fittest' policy are unlikely to transmit disease. Such divisive statements are to be deplored.

BSPA produces a helpful guide for show secretaries.

> A horse or pony is described as a skewbald or piebald by virtue of its colour, not breed, type, size or genes carried.
> Piebald: Black and white.
> Skewbald: Any other colour(s) and white – may have some black markings in addition.
> (Notes: If a horse/pony has white markings on the head, legs, belly, and/or mane and tail only, it cannot be considered a skewbald or piebald. White colour should be distributed in patches, not spots. It is desirable that the white and colour patches be evenly and symmetrically distributed. Demarkation between white and colour patches should be clearly defined and not blurred.

Overo markings, spreading upwards from the legs and belly, do tend to be more blurred. The Society does not recognise overo. Stallion licenses are naturally more complex. The British Skewbald and Piebald Association issues licenses that verify colour identification, and that the animal has undergone a veterinary examination which passed it fit for breeding and free from any apparent hereditary defects. Stallions must be two years old before examination for license.

The British Skewbald and Piebald Association was gaining over ten members weekly in 1993, when membership topped the thousand. A stud book is being set up to include both breeding and performance. The Association avoids differentiation between overo and tobiano as the former could bring in Clydesdales, and that is not the aim. The terms 'piebald' and 'skewbald' are a source of British pride, and BSPA intends to continue them.

The Northern Coloured Horse Show has held a series of successful competitions, affiliated to the British Skewbald and Piebald Association. Its venue at Cheese Vat Farm, Sheriff Hutton, York, has pleasant, open fields set in a ring of low hills.

In 1992, 40 classes were staged, with qualifiers for BSPA regional championships. That is in itself no mean achievement, for it seems only yesterday that one class for skewbalds and another for piebalds would have been the maximum. The Sheriff Hutton event began with Ponies of Native Type, followed by Brood Mares,

Registered coloured stallions at the BSPA Breeding and Performance Showcase 1993. From left, Seymour (17 hand hunter), champion Shetland Romany Paco, 1992 inhand champion Méchant, cob stallion Wolfston Amadeus, and pony stallion Romanos Pioneer.

either with foal at foot or in-foal. The Foal class was followed by Stallions or Colts. Driving Type classes were split into two: Lightweights and Tradesman's Turnouts/ Heavyweight Types. Youngstock merited separate classes for one-, two- and three-year-olds, with the winning foal able to join them for the Youngstock championship. Then came the Patchwork classes, now so popular that a division into piebalds and skewbalds was necessary. Each mustered over 20 entries, with a rosette all round, a nice touch. These classes were judged purely on the most attractive markings, not on conformation.

The Veterans class for animals fifteen years and over had a special rosette for the oldest entrant, and a trophy. The same judge, Mr Bob Ordidge MRCVS, placed the Best Condition line-up, a further stimulus to good show preparation.

Heavyweight horses came next, followed by Lightweights not exceeding or likely to exceed 14.2 hands. The Riding Pony class had the same height limit. The Cob class was for 14 to 15.1 hands, while Horses of Hunter Type had a minimum specification of 14.2 hands. There followed the White Rose trophy for the Best Inhand horse or pony.

The separate Ridden ring began with a Tack and Turnout class, then a Novice Showing for riders who had never been placed first or second in a ridden showing class, with rosettes for all competitors. Leading Rein Ponies were limited to 12.2 hands and under, this important section demonstrating that in the great majority of cases a coloured pony makes an ideal first ride. At the other end of the scale were Ridden Cobs 14 hands to 15.1 hands, with a separate class for Ridden Hunters exceeding 14.2 hands.

Ridden Native Types made an interesting category, followed by Ridden Light Horses exceeding 14.2 hands and Riding Ponies 14.2 hands and under. The Minster Trophy, named after world-famous York Minster, was awarded to the winner of the Ridden Championship. An open driving class of high quality but small numbers needs further encouragement, especially as a parti-coloured makes such a flashy driving animal.

Three jumping classes were separated on height. Working Hunter ponies of 14.2 hands and under had fences of 2 feet 9 inches maximum. Working Cobs 14 to 15.1 hands had to jump up to 2 feet 9 inches, while fences were raised to 3 feet 3 inches maximum for the Working Hunters. The Working Hunter Championship embraced all three sections.

Ridden Veterans had to be 14 years or over, either horses or ponies, and again a special rosette was awarded to the oldest. Free entry was given in the Riding for the

Charlton Checkmate, BSPA registered stallion and winner in hand.

Disabled class, open to any horse regularly used by a RDA group. The Potential RDA horse was open to all five-year-olds and over, and 15.2 hands and under. These animals were shown under saddle, with snaffle bridle but no noseband, and led off a head collar. They were judged on obedience in hand, and ridden by a lightweight adult before being led past such nuisances as balloons and banging. The Family Pony had to be ridden by all members of the family, with small jumps and hazards negotiated. The final class was a Handy Horse against the clock.

The British Skewbald and Piebald Association's third national show near Huntingdon staged an equally wide if different range of classes. The Condition and

Turnout (Ridden) was split into ponies 14.2 hands and under, and horses exceeding 14.2 hands. Lead reins were permitted, while a green arm band denoted 'grass kept'. The highest placed grass kept animal won a special rosette, its qualification being 'grass kept for more than ten months of the year'.

The Novice Showing (inhand) was for horse and handler combinations that had never won 1st, 2nd or 3rd in any showing class. The Best Child Rider was for those who had not reached their twelfth birthday, with a special prize for the best on a lead rein. Ridden Pairs were judged 50 per cent on display and manners, 10 per cent on colour, markings and match, and 10 per cent judge's discretion.

Young Handlers Inhand were divided into ten and under and eleven to fifteen. Separate classes were arranged for Best Piebald (Inhand), Part-bred Thoroughbred or Arab Inhand, Gelding Inhand and Best Rescued Inhand. Fancy Dress was for an exhibitor of any age, in hand, lead rein or ridden. Inhand and Ridden sections each had their own Championships.

The Working Showing ring staged seven classes, some subdivided. In the Green Working Hunter for horses or ponies never to have been placed, jumps were limited to 2 feet. For the Working Hunter Pony they did not exceed 2 feet 3 inches, ponies being 13 to 15 hands. Working Cobs were up to 15.1, with three inches added to the jumps, while the Working Hunter horse of over 15.1 hands had jumps up to 2 feet 9 inches.

Separate classes were provided for Riding Horse and Riding Club Horse, both of over 14.2 hands. The Family Horse started from a hand smaller, and was required to negotiate a small obstacle course to prove it to be a safe, versatile mount. Veterans Inhand were aged 16 or over, while Cobs competed to a 15.1 hands limit, with Cob Types over 15.1 hands.

Breeding classes were staged in yet another ring. They began with brood mares and foals, then six classes for yearlings, two-year-olds and three-year-olds. Colts had their own classes, with fillies and geldings combined. The Youngstock championship was followed by open classes for junior and senior stallions, the latter four years old and over.

Best Condition Inhand had similar conditions to the Ridden section, with Inhand Cobs split at 15.1 hands. Female Inhand championships and Inhand regional qualifiers finals followed.

The fourth ring began with Inhand Hunter Types and Driving Types, with a separate class for Working Hunters. 'Hairies' had their own class, being suitably encouraged. There was a special award for the best skewbald Inhand.

BSPA inhand champion 1990, Phillip Pembroke, a partbred Hanoverian stallion owned by Charles Wilson.

The British Skewbald and Piebald Association suggests that in judging a coloured class, marks be allocated as follows:

In hand

40 per cent conformation

50 per cent colour and markings

10 per cent judges' discretion

Ridden

30 per cent conformation

20 per cent colour and markings

40 per cent manners and performance

10 per cent judges' discretion

Painted Horse and Pony Society

The Painted Horse and Pony Society of Great Britain is the most recent of the three societies, set up in 1993. Its handbook states:

> In a nutshell, a 'PAINTED' horse or pony has one or more white 'PAINT' markings on its body behind a line from the base of the ear to the throatlatch, and above a line through the stifle behind and just below the elbow joint in front. The new society's aim is to provide for the selection and registration of horses and ponies with PAINT markings, but above all with good conformation, quality, soundness and performance ability. Another aim is to do away with the terms 'piebald' and 'skewbald', that have little meaning outside Britain, and to encourage all persons interested in the broken-coloured horse and pony to become totally familiar with internationally accepted terms of broken colour, namely tobiano and overo. They are based on the POSITION of the white on the body rather than the base colour.

Australia

Coloured horses are thriving in Australia. The Pinto Horse Association of New South Wales issues a comprehensive set of judges' and exhibitors' rules that are a guide to any budding organisation.

All their registered Pinto horses may be shown in either Western or English tack or equipment, unless one or the other is stipulated in the programme. All equipment and tack must be clean, well-fitting and in good repair. Exhibitors' showring attire may be of English or Western type, unless otherwise stipulated. Dress must be semi-formal, neat and clean.

No stallion or colt may be shown by any person under eighteen years of age, and must be shown in a bridle and bit or halter and chain. All stock must be sufficiently handled to be controllable in the ring. Any horse which disrupts a class and in the opinion of judge or steward is a hazard to other exhibitors or their horses will be asked to leave the ring.

Pony height must not exceed 14 hands, and horse height must exceed 14 hands, measured in both cases at the withers. The Association runs various show classes, with the rules clearly laid out. The Costume class is not a fancy dress class. All competitors must be attired in national costume, such as Spanish, Indian, Mexican, Arabian or period costume. A workout suitable to the costume is required. No workout is required for fancy dress, which is judged on presentation and appeal.

The Western Pleasure class is judged on the performance and conformation of the horse at the discretion of the judge. Horses are judged at walk, jog trot and canter, and must work both ways of the ring at all three paces. The judge must ask for the horse to be reined back. No individual workouts are required, and the rider shall not be required to dismount. Western saddle and western bridle and bits are required. Dress boots shall be western, with a western hat, suit or jeans and shirt, tie and boots. Chaps and spurs are optional.

In the English Pleasure class, the rider is instructed to have light contact on slightly loose reins. The class is judged at the walk, trot, canter, halt and reinback, to the judge's instructions, with special emphasis on well-mannered horses. Any saddle or plain snaffle bit is allowed, but no martingales, drop nosebands, whips or spurs. Informal riding attire for this class consists of hunting or felt hat, shirt and tie, hacking jacket, riding trousers or jodhpurs and boots. Individual workouts may be required.

The Open or Educated Hack Classes are judged at the walk, trot and canter, with simple or flying changes, halt, side pass, rein back or turn on the forehand as directed by the judge. Collected and extended paces may be required in these classes. Manes may be plaited or hogged. Dress should be formal or semi-formal.

The Working Stock Horse class is judged in two sections. An individual workout on a pattern is allocated a maximum of 50 points, with a further 50 points for a workout on a beast. If no cattle are available, this class may be judged solely on pattern work. Conformation does not count in this class.

Pattern Work is based on the traditional sequence of one or more figure eights at ordinary or working canter, with flying changes, and a run both ways and to the centre, each terminating in a sliding stop and turns off the hocks. The centre run ends in back ups and turning off the hocks by roll backs, pivots of 180 degrees or spins of 360 degrees. Two or three cracks of the stock whip at the walk or while stationary are obligatory.

The suggested pattern for Cattle Work is to release one beast into the arena, and have the horse steady and hold it against the arena fence, block it and turn it in the opposite direction. This is done twice, with the final turn into the centre, where the beast is circled to demonstrate control.

Breed classes in Britain are termed halter classes in Australia and America. Conformation and action true to type are sought by the Association, as defined in the Pinto Standard of Excellence. However, conformation is not considered in the Best Marked Pinto classes. Judging is purely on the Pinto markings exhibited. They seek a 50/50 ratio of colour and pattern or, alternatively, the Pinto who shows an extravagant coat pattern and stands out in a crowd. This is left to the judge's discretion.

No discrimination will be made concerning light or dark skin, or against blue, glass or dark eyes. Nor shall judges discriminate between Pinto colours. White with bay, sorrel, grey, palomino, dun, chestnut, black, roan or buckskin are equally acceptable. There are only two colour patterns, tobiano and overo, with wide variations in colour and area. No discrimination will be made concerning tobiano and overo patternings – they are of equal value.

'While colour and markings are not primarily determinative factors in judging, it must be borne in mind that where two horses are equal in all other qualities of conformation, quality, action, presentation and performance, the award should be made to the entry which more closely represents the Pinto horse and is more readily recognisable as a Pinto', says the Association.

Presentation alone is considered in the Best Presented classes. Conformation is not considered, only the way the horse is turned out and presented. The Junior Handler classes are judged on the showmanship and presentation of the handler exhibiting the horse to the judge.

Hoofs should be dressed to show their natural colour and markings. Striped hoofs are a Pinto characteristic, and must not be penalised. Any change of colour or markings other than the hoof is prohibited. No dyes or bleaches may be used. Stains may be removed by accepted washing methods only. Horses may be shown with natural, trimmed or plaited manes and tails.

It is the tradition of the show ring that riders and drivers be correctly attired for the class in question, that attendants be neatly dressed and horses properly presented. Protective headgear for riders is compulsory.

'Good judging depends on a correct observance of the fine points and the selection of the best horses for the purpose described by conditions of the class', says the Association. 'A judge serves three interests: his own conscience, exhibitors, and spectators. He should make clear to the audience that the best horses win. Onlookers often pay to get in and they want to understand what happens'.

7   Buying a coloured horse

It is one thing to admire coloured horses from the safety of the ringside, or in someone else's field or stable. It is quite another to fork out hard cash for an animal that might go lame as soon as you arrive home, or prove less trustworthy than anticipated. These strictures apply to any horse, so why should buying a coloured be any different? Basically it is not; the same rules of general soundness, even temperament and good manners apply.

The first difficulty is to find your animal. Sales are advertised far and wide and at regular intervals for Thoroughbreds, Cleveland Bays, performance horses, Shires and hunters, children's ponies and show jumpers. Specialist sales under recognised auctioneers are just starting for coloured horses, and large numbers are also gathered together at such Fairs as Appleby in Cumbria (pages 65–71).

Rule Number One is to take an expert with you, unless you really are one yourself. Then have in mind the type of horse or pony you want: approximate height, build and colour, and whether hairy or clean-legged. Consider how readily the horse would sell again. Though this applies to all horses, it is important in a parti-coloured because of points generally absent in other types. You may not mind a light eye, but some buyers object, and a dealer would immediately point this out if you were trying to sell, though not of course if you were buying!

Coloured mare and foal in the sale ring in North Yorkshire.

The type of horse you want: the author assesses the height of a possible purchase.

Showing his paces under the hammer.

Most people like the eye itself to be set in colour. This can vary from a dark face to 'spectacles' of colour around the eye, or even a dark eyelid. An eye against a purely white background tends to look less attractive. Also, a dark eye is less often found against a white background; this usually preferred dark eye tends to go with a coloured surround. However, if the rest of the animal is pleasing, you may decide to overlook what is regarded by others as detrimental. You may usefully bring the fact into play as a bargaining counter.

The body colour should show nice sharp divisions, especially in a tobiano. An overo's white spreading upwards from legs and belly does tend to mingle into the solid colour. Tobiano markings should be well broken about the body, but should not be 'bitty'. One that is nearly all either white or solid coloured apart from a very few markings is often less desirable than a horse that is 50 per cent white and 50 per cent coloured. The shading referred to may come as the animal ages, and a sharp

A light eye set in colour. Freezebranding is a good policy in addition to the coloured's 'built in' identification pattern.

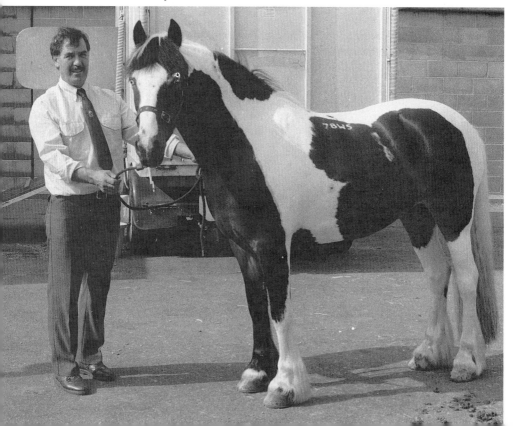

divide on a yearling may be less distinct in five years' time. If an eight-year-old mare has clear markings, she will be in demand as a brood mare, but obviously at an enhanced price.

Some people like two colours on mane or tail. The colours here are not inter-mixed hair for hair, but are in streaks or stripes. Again, this is a purely personal factor. A dark tail on a horse that is half and half black or chestnut and white can really set it off.

As with any horse, the more white there is, the harder it is to keep clean! Greys that go lighter with age tend to be less popular for this reason, and a piebald with jet black markings seems to show up any shortcomings on the white parts if they are not really clean. Perhaps that counts against the coloureds, but nothing like as much as when three or four of them have been rolling in a wet field and come in resembling solid coloured horses!

A dark hoof is an asset. Farriers prefer them, and claim that these dark hooves are stronger. However, coloured horses do tend to have sound feet. They may also have stripes on the hooves, and this is no detriment whatever in a coloured. In fact, it is a characteristic.

The amount of feather is a purely personal choice. Long mane, tail and feather are beloved by the travelling people, and many who drive prefer hairy legs. For riding or jumping, cleaner legs may be desirable. The point is that you can take the feather off, but you can't put it back on, at least for several months until it has grown again. One friend with a piebald stallion that we very much admired, a medium height chunky chap, had masses of feather, but customers seeking riding pony offspring didn't approve, so it was clipped off. That's a reminder to check whether the clean leg is natural or shaven. Taking the hair off a strong skewbald is sacrilege to many, but the customer is always right.

'Coloured Hunter, 16 hands 1 in., skewbald, 6 years, gelding. Middle/Heavy-weight. Placed X-country, SJ. Hunted last season. Sensible, kind, good to shoe, box, clip and traffic. £7,000.' This *Horse and Hound* advertisement in autumn 1991 indicates the rise in values of a good, well-broken parti-coloured horse. The South of England vendor was not sure whether the colour affected the interest in this instance; the horse was principally a hunter, of the size that always commands a premium, and the fact that he possessed very clear and distinct markings may not have greatly affected the issue. Suffice to say that, a few years ago, a coloured hunter might have been sold at a discount.

This skewbald's patches were dark brown, his tail black. Taken to the sea for the

95

first time, with the waves crashing about him, he didn't bat an eyelid. He was traffic-proof and stoic; when being bandaged or having bandages removed, he just 'stood there'. The owner trimmed off some of his feather.

In the rest of this chapter, Audrey Hart describes her first venture in purchasing a coloured horse.

Broken to ride and drive! How on earth could that be? She was only a two-year-old. I stood gaping at this gorgeous animal, clutching the catalogue and listening to the seller talking of her virtues to a prospective buyer. 'Been ridden by my ten-year-old son: no problems! Driven around the streets of Carlisle by the same boy: no problems!'

Was I hearing correctly? I wonder how many folk would trust a ten-year-old boy to a two-year-old filly in Carlisle, or a two-year-old filly to a ten-year-old boy, for that matter?

Audrey Hart's Queenie in the Victorian Hayride at Walkington, Yorkshire.

Queenie later produced a splendid foal.

I was standing by a pen during Wigton market's October sale. Inside was a piebald. She was 14.3 hands, strongly built, heavy boned and was a striking colour, about 80 per cent white and 20 per cent black.

Certainly she seemed kind, as people walked in and out of her stall, prodding and poking, lifting feet, looking at teeth, eyes and ears, picking up her tail and feeling her legs. She was by a black Clydesdale stallion out of a skewbald pony mare, and she was lovely.

And I was looking for a horse. I'd always liked coloured horses. I also love heavy horses, but would certainly not dream of buying a purebred. I wanted a female, and preferably a young horse to train on. It all seemed too good to be true.

Now, one thing was certainly true, and that was that I didn't (and still don't) know enough to buy an unknown horse at a public auction, and I needed help. There were about 180 lots to go before her turn. I had a little time and so I scoured the sale. Fortunately a number of my horsey friends were there. One after another

Queenie's filly foal, Dazzler, by HIS stallion Dixi.

they were asked if they would go and look at the filly. One after another they came back with their reports, which all added up to approval. I wanted her, and if I had the money, I was to go ahead. The more experienced gave me a price limit. It was higher than I expected, but if I did this, that and the other, financially I could manage.

Nerve. I needed nerve. My knees were a bit wobbly as she was led from her pen and joined the queue for the sale ring. The ringside was so packed that I wondered if I'd ever be through the crowd in time for her turn. I was. My throat was parched and dry. She was next. The gate opened and the ten-year-old boy rode her in, no saddle or bridle, only a headcollar. She walked proudly round and round. I was fascinated. So fascinated, I had almost forgotten about the bidding. It had raced away and I began to wonder what was happening.

The bidding stopped suddenly, at £100 more than my 'ceiling'. The reports from my advisers rang in my ears. The sight of her proud walk filled my eyes. I bid. My first bid, and I knew it would be my last. There was a silence. The auctioneer broke it, cajoling others to bid. But they didn't, and she was mine.

Later, after a mad dash to arrange transport, and following a visit to a building society in town and complicated discussions at a bank, she was paid for. I found her tied up in a pen in a corner of the market, and stood by her, listening with some pride to comments of passers-by. One man even tried to buy her from me. He had apparently missed the sale and brandished fistfuls of ten pound notes. But she was mine and not for sale.

Luckily, I caught sight of the vendors just as they were leaving the market. I deluged them with questions. They were as helpful as they could be. 'What's her name?' No one had mentioned it. I was told she had been named by 'grandfather' after the best horse he had ever had, and he had thought she might come as good as that one, one day. I hope so, my Queenie.

8   Spotlight on horses and people

I asked a number of experienced horse people how they regarded coloured horses.

'They always seem to be sound of foot and sound of constitution', said Roger Clark. 'Coloured horses have never been numerous in this part of Suffolk: numbers have kept steady during my lifetime.'

Both master farriers, Roger and his wife Cheryl farm with horses only. 'It's a funny thing about coloureds; they always seem outstanding. I don't know whether that is because they really do dominate the best positions, or whether they are simply more eye-catching with their striking colours', said Roger Clark. When I spoke to him one dull November evening, he had just returned from hunting the Essex and Suffolk foxhounds. 'We had a girl out today on a coloured pony, and she always seemed well up', he said. 'Another odd thing is that a coloured horse with a white leg may have a blue foot. As farriers we appreciate the hard blue hoof.'

As a small boy Roger Clark saw a gypsy horse that was shod with a conventional shoe held on by wire nails! Instead of being clinched in the usual way, these nails

Farriers usually find sound feet on a coloured.

were held down by half-inch wire netting staples, which did the job. 'That must have been some foot!' he said.

Mike Flood of Skeyton, Norwich, is chairman of the Eastern Counties Heavy Horse Association. His work with an agricultural engineering firm takes him all over East Anglia. He recalled William Peeke, who started working with horses as a lad at Lacy's Farm, Worstead, Norwich. The very first he owned was three-quarters heavy, and coloured. Its job was patching roads by the old molten tar and stone method.

The tar was heated in a metal vessel on iron wheels, with a single wheel in front. There was a fire in the grate below the 'copper' barrel of tar, and a chimney above. A single horse pulled the contraption with a pair of shafts. The driver poured molten tar into holes in the road, and another horse and cart carrying crushed stone chippings followed, making up the holes on top of the tar. Obviously, idiot horses would have been quite out of place in this essential work that kept roads usable for decades.

William Peeke extended his business until he had twenty coloured horses, drivers and carts. 'He always said that his luck would hold as long as he had a coloured horse', Mike Flood recalled. 'He worked his horses seriously until 1976. The odd thing was that in the year he sold his last coloured horse, he died aged 82. Engraved on his gravestone are a pair of horses and a plough.'

Mike Flood has a lasting regret. William Peeke offered him a coloured yearling colt out of a big coloured mare for £350. He didn't take it. 'I've often wished since that I had bought that horse', stressed Mike Flood, who drives a heavy team in ploughing matches. 'The public loves to see big, powerful coloured horses. A coloured stallion that William Peeke ran for two or three seasons before gelding him is grandsire to my bay horse Bowler.'

These coloured horses owned by William Peeke were all big, the size of Shires. He had grazing on thirty acres of marsh at Ruston Common, and ran his colts there. They must have been a fine sight on the level grassland.

William Peeke liked the Romany type of people, and was a regular at fairs such as Barnett and Devizes. From them he obtained the big, attractive coloured horses that earned him his daily bread.

Pictures from the early part of the nineteenth century show teams of piebald dray horses owned by the great brewing houses, according to the *Livestock Journal* of May 1899. Scenes of brew house yards and the like were favourite subjects with animal painters, who found in the splendid horses to be seen there attractive subjects for the brush.

Ever ready for controversy, the Journal found that the liking for horses with coats of this curious mixture of colours gives direct contradiction to the theory held by some that 'composite coloured' horses such as piebalds, skewbalds, black and white, or chestnut and white are, as a rule, soft and unreliable for hard work. These alleged links between colours and hardiness are by no means confined to the horse world; breeders of Blackfaced sheep aver that lighter-faced ones are less hardy, without any proper study.

In the old coaching days coachmasters affected teams which included one piebald or skewbald in the lead; the odd-coloured horse was always one that could trot while the rest were galloping, to the end that if a charge of furious driving were preferred the offending coachman could call his outside passengers to witness that one horse was trotting. This demonstrates that the parti-coloured, besides being noticeable in daylight and particularly in darkness, had admirable trotting action, or it would not have kept up with the rest.

In some parts of the country superstition invests the parti-coloured horse with a halo of good fortune, it being considered 'lucky' to meet him. Some years ago a correspondent of *The Field*, who rode a skewbald gelding in London, wrote to enquire why small boys, when he passed them, shouted at the 'lucky horse', and invariably made a cross on the toe of each boot with a finger-tip sucked for the purpose.

He does not appear to have found anyone capable of explaining this social phenomenon. 'In 1899 the piebald harness horse is reserved to the advertiser's van and the circus; and the fashion in circus horses during the last fifteen or twenty years seems to have changed to a great extent in favour of less conspicuously coloured animals', he said.

He continued: 'The writer had penned the above sentence and happened to glance out of the window in response to a note of a coach horn, to see the Brighton coach swinging along behind as smart a team of piebalds as whip need wish to handle; and as if to confirm a previous remark, comes another coach with a piebald conspicuous as the near leader.'

Inheritance of the piebald coat when one parent is a bay, brown or otherwise plain-coloured, appears to be uncertain, states this correspondent of almost 100 years ago. He cites Professor Cosser Ewart,

> in his highly interesting, suggestive book *The Penicuik Experiments*. He mentions the case of an Iceland skewbald pony used in his telegony experiments.

Professor Ewart's experiments with breeding from a skewbald Icelandic mare: her foal by a Zebra stallion and her foal by a bay Shetland pony.

She first threw a light bay foal to an Iceland sire; next, to the zebra stallion Matopo, a hybrid foal, which was dark dun, indistinctly striped, but without the smallest patch of white; and, thirdly, to a bay Shetland pony a piebald foal 'almost the exact image of herself'.

Another slant on colour beliefs comes from Sir Garrard Tyrwhitt-Drake, writing in *The Horseman's Year* (1949).

Coloured horses, piebalds and skewbalds, I was always told as a small boy, brought luck if you passed one and did not see its tail. I don't know the origin of this superstition, but the writer of a letter in the *Daily Express* in 1922 seemed to have heard a very different account of the bad and good luck of this horse.

One Samuel Phillips, who appeared in a police Court on a charge of working an unfit horse, pleaded: 'I intended to have the horse killed, because I believe piebalds bring me bad luck.'

Sir Garrard continued:

Probably the most famous piebald, even if he was only legendary, was 'Sharaty', the charger of King Marko of Serbia, who brought good fortune to his master, his country and to whomever they went to help.

Though an experienced and observant horse breeder, Sir Garrard disclaimed theoretically or scientifically procured knowledge, but based his remarks entirely on practical experience. They are cogent enough to repeat.

Coloured horses out of or by coloured horses are easy to breed, but it must be borne in mind that a coloured horse lacks pigment, and to be certain of breeding a good piebald it is advisable that one only of the parents is a piebald and the other a black with white points (star and stockings), otherwise one is very likely to get a brown and white. In the same way two brown and whites will often produce a bay and white, or even a chestnut and white.

I am often asked how one can be sure of breeding a horse of a certain colour. I always reply, 'One can never be certain, but one can be very certain how one will NOT.' As I have found it, the amount of pigment colouration in the parents is all-important and, generally speaking, especially in odd-coloured horses, the pigment of the foal is more often than not less than in the parents. Certain coloured horses are often very productive in reproducing progeny of the same colour as themselves. Grey is a very predominant colour, so is the dun with black stripe down the back, and often small stripes across the back of the front legs, above the knee. Blue roans and red roans often produce their colour. A red roan stallion at stud near Maidstone produced over 90 per cent of red roan foals, but against this a roan (neither blue nor red) which I put to my cream pony stallion produced a pure cream foal!

Colour breeding in horses is a lottery. One can never be sure of obtaining a certain result, even when one uses sires and dams that should produce what is wanted, but be very sure that if a coloured horse is required it won't be obtained from a grey.

That last statement is at variance with modern gypsies' views; some among them recommend a grey as one parent of parti-coloureds. A geneticist would probably say that some greys of the good Sir Garrard's experience were homozygous for grey, and so would indeed produce nothing but greys to horses of any other solid colour. Some of his other experiences may also be simply explained by an understanding of dominant and recessive characters, but we should always note the practical man's views.

On the merits of odd-coloured horses, Sir Garrard was emphatic:

I don't think anybody, whether they knew one end of a horse from the other or not, will dispute the fact that an 'odd' coloured horse is attractive and does catch the eye.

The proof of the pudding is in the eating, and the circus proprietors – and they are no mean showmen – have adopted these horses from the time of Astley and 'Lord' George Sanger right up to Bertram Mills and the present-day circus proprietors, because they make every one take notice.

What is an odd-coloured horse? There are many examples, piebalds and skewbalds or, as the circus man describes them, black-and-white and red-and-white respectively – blue roan and white, cream-and-white, spots and pure cream.

The Pieman

One of the few parti-coloured hunters of the 1970s was The Pieman. He carried Lord Middleton as Field Master of the Middleton Hunt in North Yorkshire for some ten or twelve seasons.

The Pieman was by the Thoroughbred Pinocchio by Pinza. He is illustrated here at Farlington in the Vale of York in 1972. He stood 16 hands and was bought from Lady Susan Watson, daughter of Lord Halifax.

'As Field Master I needed something that would perform', recalled Lord Middleton. 'The Pieman was absolutely brilliant and would keep going all day; the best horse I ever had. He was a very bold jumper; I never knew him refuse.'

Though retired when aged eighteen, that was not the end of The Pieman's

Lord Middleton and The Pieman hunting in Yorkshire in 1972.

hunting career. One day hounds ran to his paddock at Birdsall, Malton, and the old black and white gelding jumped out and crossed one of the fish ponds to join them. He was found dead in his paddock of a heart attack two or three years later.

Mancha

A. F. Tschiffely made one of mankind's great rides through 10,000 miles of the Americas, including unmapped, trackless country. He used two horses, one of which, Mancha, was a skewbald. At the time it seemed pure chance, but Tschiffely cannot have been displeased, for he recalled another, his first pony.

> He was a lovely chap, a golden-red and snow-white skewbald with a bristly mane, proud fiery eyes and a long flowing tail. Where he was bought, and how much he cost, I never bothered to ask; not out of politeness, for in those days of my early childhood I didn't know that one must not look a gift horse in the mouth.
>
> What a wonderful beast he was; his manners were perfect, and despite the somewhat wild look in his eyes, he was so quiet and docile that alongside him even the proverbially quiet little lamb would have been frisky.
>
> After my father had lifted me on to his back, he stood stock-still, and only moved a little when I gingerly asked him to do so. The thrill of it; my father, mother, sisters and brother looking on as I showed off, sitting on my own horse!

Later, A. F. Tschiffely gave Mancha the following words: 'If you had seen me when I was a colt you would probably have thought I looked very funny, for my coat was all dark red and white blotches, and I had a short, scraggy tail and long legs, like four animated stilts.'

This unpromising start developed into a saga unique in equine history. Together with Gato, Mancho carried his master and pack nearly 10,000 miles the length of the American continent. The pair were South American Creoles or Criollos. They are the descendants of a few horses brought to the Argentine in 1535 by Don Pedro Mendoza, founder of the city of Buenos Aires. These animals were of the finest Spanish stock, at that time the best in Europe, with a large admixture of Arab and Barb blood in their veins. That these were the first horses in America since pre-history is borne out by history, by tradition, and by the fact that no native American dialect contains a word for a horse.

Later, when Buenos Aires was sacked by the Indians and its inhabitants massacred, the descendants of the Spaniards' horses were abandoned to wander over the country. Drought, treacherous climate with sudden temperature changes, Indians and wild animals killed off all but the strongest. The Creole horses have since performed marches that would appear incredible were they not established facts.

Criollo breeder Dr Emilo Solanet gave these two horses to Tschiffely when he heard of the proposed ride. 'They were the wildest of the wild. To break them had taxed the powers of several of the best "domadores" for some time, and even when I took them over they were far from tame', said Tschiffely.

> Mancha was 16, and even now (at 22) will not allow anyone except myself to saddle him. To a European horse lover they would appear, to put it mildly, curious. Mancha is a red, with heavy irregular splashes of white; white face and stockings. Gato is more or less a coffee colour, a sort of a cross between a bay

Mancha reunited with Gato and A. F. Tschiffely.

and a dun, or what the American cowboys used to call a 'buckskin'. Their sturdy legs, short thick necks and Roman noses are far removed from the points of a first-class English hunter.

At journey's end, Tschiffely and the pair had to part. He gave them lumps of sugar; they softly nickered into his ears, asking for more. For a long time he sat, then galloped away on another horse. Before long he reined in his mount, turned in his saddle and called: 'Good-bye, Mancha and Gato!'

This was not the end, for fifteen years later the trio were reunited. Even after that interval, Mancha and Gato remembered the snap of Tschiffely's fingers when he bent down, as he did in the wilds many times a day. Up came a fore or a hind leg, to check for stones or loose shoes, just as in the old days on the long, long trail. Though both horses were well over thirty, they looked fresh and fit after a retirement on the Argentine pampas never better earned. Mancha deserves his place among the all-time broken-coloured 'greats'.

Tschiffely was later able to write: 'Thanks to my two horses' demonstration of resistance and hardiness, the Criollo breed – which a quarter of a century ago threatened to disappear – flourishes throughout South America, where breeders take a great interest in the type of animals of which my two companions were such typical specimens.'

Hercules

Drum horses tend to develop pretty strong characters, and none more so than the tall piebald Charlie. His official name was Hercules, and as such he was publicly known as the great Drum Horse of his generation. He featured on an army first day cover, while postcards depicting the sights of London often had four Blues and Royals trumpeters – and Charlie. He would listen to talk, every bit as nosey as a human being. Corporal Major Peter Marsh, who rode him, said: 'Charlie's not my horse; he's my friend.'

Men of the Blues and Royals all say there will never be another Charlie. After Hannibal, he became their senior Drum Horse during the 1970s. He had a terrific sense of duty, yet on every Trooping of the Colour ceremony near Buckingham Palace while awaiting HM the Queen Mother, he kept looking over his shoulder to his friends in the crowd. He had an uncanny knack of locating those he loved.

He would none the less play tricks on them. At one stage he had a groom, Tony

Plank, whom he adored. Tony was a last-minute, rather disorganised man, and Charlie added to his discomforture. Two essentials, the blacking brush, or Tony's own hat, would be missing. Tony would search high and low, until the meaning of Charlie's innocent expression dawned, and the missing items were retrieved from the manger.

Charlie was always superbly looked after, spotlessly clean, his tack immaculate. He adored being groomed and having his mane combed, yet every so often would decide against it. He would jerk his head higher and higher, out of reach, and turn it from side to side to side. Then suddenly he would flop against the wall with his front legs crossed and his head practically on his knees.

Hercules the Drum Horse, known at home as Charlie, with Trooper Tony Plank, preparing for the Horse of the Year Show in 1973.

He was not so keen on Geoff Blogg, with whom he had a mutual antipathy. Before the Personalities Parade at Wembley he would rear and buck, very nasty for the drummer who is held on by the drums; he just cannot come off.

Geoff and Charlie were in a Horse of the Year Show parade, following the trumpet horses into the arena. The idea was for the trumpet horses to hive off two and two on either side, and the drum horse to make a beeline down the middle. Instead, Charlie did a bending race in and out of the line of eight fir trees, leaving Geoff speechless with shame and fury. The audience of course thought it was part of the show, but Geoff's colleagues hurt their sides laughing.

In another parade, Charlie could have been forgiven for mishaps. Yet he loved his rider, John Frew, pushed into an unaccustomed role. John was paralysed by nerves, and forgot the basic rule of foot reins – that when one is pulled the other is released. The result was that Charlie stayed motionless with his head hard into his chest; he had every excuse for playing up, but John was a friend. The officer noticed, came over and gently pushed John's leg forward, whereupon Charlie gratefully stretched his neck. Despite his discomfort he would willingly have stood throughout the performance with his head on his chest, rather than unsettle John.

Above all else, Charlie disliked the Pony Club games, and he was scheduled to enter the arena after them, endure the drumming of feet from the grandstand above, and have the ponies screech past him on their exit. This did not help preparations. Yet he enjoyed the Spanish Riding School, and watched their every movement very, very carefully.

The drum horses often took exercise through the old Covent Garden. Charlie loved cauliflowers, and would be liable to snatch a net with his strong teeth.

He was remarkably quick on the uptake. After a week of solid rain at Haverford-west Musical Ride, the last evening performance ended. The troop was due to pull out next morning, but the commanding officer suddenly decided that if they could pull off in two hours they could go straight home. Charlie quickly realised what was happening, and boxed himself. 'You never worried about specific commands with Charlie. You just talked to him as you would another human being,' declared his grooms.

Time and Chance

Time and Chance are two 11 hands piebald ponies owned by Anne Vasey of Grits Farm, Weaverthorpe, Malton, East Riding. They were saved from the meat man's

111

Anne Vasey driving Time (*right*) and Chance to qualify in the 1988 Lombard Double Harness Scurry.

yard in 1983, and during breaking went through every hedge on the place, yet in 1986 gained reserve championship at Wembley in the Lombard Double Harness Scurry.

'We understand they had been just pets for an elderly lady in Bedfordshire', said Anne Vasey. 'They qualified via ten shows, and Chance, the daughter, was a seven-year-old at Wembley, and her mother Time was ten. They were beaten by Julie Blake's palomino and white pair Touch and Go.'

Commentator Raymond Brooks-Ward described Anne Reid (as she then was) as 'scurry driving's Nigel Mansell!' The ponies are believed to be Welsh cross Shetland, and the one time they were parted Chance almost broke her neck, so they have lived together ever since. The Vasey family saved another parti-coloured six-month-old pony from slaughter, and at five years old Tania has developed into an ideal children's pony.

The coloured horse in literature and art

Legend

Though we may speculate on the origins of the first piebalds and skewbalds, no supposition can match Ilse Mirus's story, 'The Legend of the Odd-Coloured Horses', translated by Daphne Goodall from *Hufschlag Erklang* (1960).

St Nicholas wandered the length and breadth of Russia, helping those with troubles. One day a celestial messenger appeared, begging him to go quickly to Nikita Cathedral, where the Advent service was under threat from the wicked giant Arius.

'I'll start today', said St Nicholas. He was allotted the best coachman, Wassilij, who harnessed up his three horses one behind the other. The leader was a very small white pony. In the middle was a coal-black horse, with an active brown mare between the shafts.

They drove for many nights and days, until at last they broke their journey at a coaching house within range of Nikita Cathedral. But Arius had heard of this, and threatened his servants with death if they did not slow St Nicholas down for a day or two. The landlord of the inn was rude and sullen, and claimed that all the oats were used up, but Nicholas told Wassilij to take the sack out from under the seat, and when he shook it into the manger a stream of golden corn poured out. The travellers ate, prayed, and went to sleep.

At midnight, Wassilij got up to check the horses. He returned pale and shaking. 'Father Nicholas, come with me to the stable, and see what a terrible misfortune has befallen us.'

> The horses were lying all over the place, chopped up into pieces: there some legs, there the heads, somewhere else the neck and quarters . . . Wassilij began to cry. They had been such lovely horses.

The Holy Man said kindly: 'It's all right, Wassilij. Come, put the horses together – so, just as they were.' Wassilij did as he was told, joining the heads to the necks, necks to legs and so on. The three horses 'sprang to their feet, as well and lively as if nothing had happened, shook their manes, danced around and nuzzled into their corn'.

They set off again before dawn. But as it got lighter, Wassilij kept leaning forward, peering at the horses. 'It seems to me they have become different colours. Originally they were of plain colours but now they're chequered like calves. Surely in my hurry in the dark I didn't put the wrong pieces together? That would be awful.'

St Nicholas answered: 'Don't worry. They can stay like that. Get on with the driving so that we don't arrive too late.'

When they arrived, the service had already started, and St Nicholas hurried to the altar steps, to find Arius standing there. The powerful giant began to shake, had a convulsive fit, and died without Confession.

Since then, the legend tells us, coachmen have always used piebald or skewbald horses. 'And everyone knows quite well that such horses have the strongest lungs and that their legs are like iron.'

Literature

The Irish RM

Not all coloured horses are angels. Somerville and Ross, in the entirely delightful *Further Experiences of an Irish RM*, found one that was definitely not. The RM and his wife Philippa were marooned at a friend's, awaiting their hunters, and unable to proceed to the meet.

> 'The master sent me to ask you, sir, if you'd like to have the pony-phaeton to drive down to the station to meet the half-past ten train. Flavin might be sending the horses on it, and it'd save you time to meet them there.' We closed on the offer . . . We presently seated ourselves in it, low down behind an obese piebald pony, with a pink nose, and a mane hogged to the height of its ears. As I took up the whip it turned and regarded us with an unblinkered eye, pink-lidded and small as a pig's . . .
>
> The mud was deep, and the piebald pony plodded through it at a sullen jog. The air was mild and chilly, like an uninteresting woman; . . . it hardly seemed worthwhile to beat the pony when he sank into a walk . . .
>
> The gates stood wide open, and the pony turned in as by an accustomed route, and crawled through them with that simulation of complete exhaustion that is the gift of lazy ponies . . .

On either side of the narrow drive laurels and rhododendrons were crammed as thickly as they could be planted . . . The tunnel ran uphill, and I drove the pony up it as one drives a hoop, by incessant beating; had I relaxed my efforts he would probably, like a hoop, have lain down . . .

Divining the determination of the piebald pony to die, if necessary, rather than pass a hall door without stopping at it, yet debarred by the decencies from thrashing him past the long line of windows, I administered two or three rousing tugs at his wooden mouth. At the third tug the near rein broke. The pony stopped dead . . . Simultaneously the hall door was flung open . . .

The young lady aimed her glasses at the piebald, motionless in sullen stupor, and replied irrelevantly: 'Why, that's the Knoxes' pony! . . . Do come in! . . . The pony's all right – he'll sleep there for months, he always does.'

While the party was taking tea, a sound of wheels was heard on the gravel drive. Emerging, the visitors found 'nothing there save a complicated pattern of arcs and angles on the gravel, as of a four-wheeled vehicle that has taken an uncommonly short turn. At the bend of the avenue the pony-carriage, our link with the world without, was disappearing from view, the piebald pony heading for home at a piglike but determined gallop.'

National Velvet

One of the most famous coloured horses in fiction was The Piebald, immortalised in Enid Bagnold's *National Velvet*, and made into a film starring Elizabeth Taylor and Micky Rooney. Ridden by Velvet in the Grand National in the days before lady jockeys were accepted, The Piebald was one of four that survived a monumental pile-up.

The fourteen-year-old Velvet and her friend Mi Taylor – her father's slaughterhouse employee – had connived in the deception. But they had not anticipated the fame of a win.

There was a powder-puff called 'The Velvet', in gold letters on printed voile, and a mechanical piebald horse that wound up and hopped across the floor. There was a cartoon in one of the evening papers of Velvet coming over Becher's sitting between the wings of Pegasus, and all the other horses looking scared. It was called 'The Unseen Adversary'. There were marvellous love letters from strangers, and boys at school, and workmen. One of the best begin 'Divine Equestrian'.

It was all a long haul from an early gymkhana. Velvet read out: '"Children (Novice) Jumping." Me on Sir Pericles . . . and on the piebald.'

'The piebald!' The three voices snapped in the stall like whipcracks. 'The piebald! But you've never ridden him.'
  'I shall have ridden him. By then. Remember how he jumped the wall? . . . We'll take Sir Pericles and change the saddles. His ought to fit the piebald. There's nothing wrong with the piebald, except that he hated being shut in square fields with walls. Or else he likes jumping walls.'

Soon afterwards he escaped again. 'He came down the village street, slipping and sliding and snorting and his eyes shining.' 'He's like a prince!' said Velvet.

Allen Seaby

Among the more observant and accurate writers of children's books after World War One was Allen W. Seaby. He wrote delightful pony stories, of which two are relevant to our theme. One was *Skewbald, The New Forest Pony*, published in 1923:

One hot June afternoon, a group of ponies with their foals and yearlings stood on the edge of a tableland or 'plain' in the New Forest. The ground about them was covered with stunted heather and fern, with here and there patches of moss and bare white gravel showing the poverty of the soil . . .
  Perhaps the most striking in colour of the group on the hill was a chestnut mare, of that rich hue known as 'liver' chestnut. In the sun her coat flashed bright orange-red; . . . her foal at the moment was lying in the heather, out of sight . . .
  But the interesting thing about him was his colour, for he was a 'skewbald', patterned boldly in chestnut and white. Nearly all the other foals were dark, and it was as yet almost impossible to foretell their exact adult colour. Alone among the youngsters, the skewbald foal showed what his coat would be like when he was full grown.

Allen W. Seaby tells of another 'piebald' episode in *Sheltie: The Story of a Shetland Pony*. Sheltie and another yearling were on the sea shore of one of the group of islands after which they were named.

One day at low tide they enjoyed the warmth of the sun-baked rocks and, feeling drowsy, lay down and dozed. The piebald did not waken properly until a splash of cold water fell on her nose. Then she heard her mother and others calling shrilly. They prepared to leave. But what was this? The rock was no longer joined to the land; there was no causeway now, only a surging channel between them and the mainland.

The piebald's mother came down to the sea edge, stood knee-deep in the water and whinnied loudly to her yearling. The piebald understood. She began to wade into the sea, and her companion followed. For a time they kept their feet, but the current was too strong for them.

They struck out gallantly as if they were experienced swimmers, not attempting to swim directly to shore, but letting themselves be carried to a low peninsula jutting out from the land.

Presently the piebald felt a hoof touch something hard. She had reached firm ground. Splashing more and more as they rose higher, the two at last gained the shore. They shook their coats like dogs, sending showers of water which made the other ponies, who had followed their passage with interest, shrink back. It was the piebald's first and last swim.

Verse

Earlier this century Patrick Chalmers delighted in the parti-coloured ponies of his childhood. Here's how he felt *After the Circus*:

When the Circus came to town
There came steeds of high renown –
Horses black and white and brown,
Horses fairy-tale and tall;
Each had coat like diamond stone is,
Each one stepped like ceremonies;
But I liked the piebald ponies
Best of all;

117

I liked the piebald ponies
Best of all.

Some folks dream of fairyland;
Some of pirates, tarred and tanned;
But there's sugar in my hand
In the dream I dream about,
Which of boxes, rows and rows, is
All my stud, the dream supposes,
And from each a piebald nose is
Looking out,
Looking out;
And from each a piebald nose is
Looking out.

Art

Animal painters in the heyday of British sporting art in the eighteenth and nine-teenth centuries tended to concentrate on coach horses, hunters and racehorses. As artists they had a living to make, so naturally turned to the more lucrative outlets and wealthier clients who could indulge their fancies.

As we have seen, broken-coloured Thoroughbreds, and therefore hunters and racehorses, were in a very tiny minority, so there are few painted examples. Among coach horses, a grey or piebald assisted both the coachmen and any oncoming vehicles on a murky night.

Stella Walker's *Sporting Art: England 1700–1900* (1972) contains the expected greys in coaching teams, including a beautiful near-wheeler and off-leader among chestnuts, by Charles Cooper Henderson. The R. G. Reeve print after James Pollard shows a speedy piebald at its best. Named 'The Taglioni Windsor Coach', this 11⅛ by 16 in. aquatint was published by J. Watson in 1837, and credited to Fores of London.

Stella Walker points out that James Pollard's career coincided with both the brief coaching era and the introduction of the aquatint, which enabled his work to be spread more widely. The author mentions Pollard's 'neat, unruffled horses, teams perhaps *too* well matched, leaders and wheelers moving in exact symmetry', as indeed we see here.

The Taglioni Windsor Coach', painted by James Pollard and engraved by R. G. Reeve.

Sally Mitchell's *Dictionary of British Equestrian Artists* (1985) has a few marvellous piebalds and skewbalds. There's a magnificent black, chestnut and white by Alfred de Dreux, 'An Arab Stallion near a Fence'. This 32½ x 40 in. painting is signed and dated 1857. 'A fierceness seldom captured by English painters', says Sally Mitchell.

De Dreux, who lived from 1810 to 1860, painted in both France and England, and specialised in horses. Sally Mitchell includes another of his works, 'Out Exercising', a signed 7 x 13 in. watercolour. Two of the five finely depicted horses are skewbalds. De Dreux made great play of light on his horses' coats, and possibly favoured broken colours for this reason. We shall never know. He was killed in a duel in 1860 by Comte Fleury, Napoleon's aide-de-camp.

The most fascinating work for coloured horse enthusiasts among Sally Mitchell's 640 reproductions is 'The Coloured Team' by Albert Clark. This Victorian artist has depicted four marvellously sharp piebalds, the sort many of us dream about. One is flicking an impatient heel at an aggravating little prick-eared terrier; the horses wait, full of spirit, to cross to the coach house. 'These slightly stubby round jointed little horses are typical of the horses Clark normally portrayed', says Sally Mitchell.

George Henry Laporte's 'Dover–London Royal Mail' is signed and dated 1850. It shows the wheelers trotting while the leaders are cantering. 'Lovely movement in

'The Coloured Team' by Albert Clark. Oil on canvas.

'Dover to London Royal Mail' by G. H. Laporte.

the coloured horse', says Sally Mitchell. 'To be within speed regulations at least one horse had to be trotting, therefore a trotter was frequently used as a wheeler, as a trotter could trot at a speed at which other horses galloped.' Laporte (1802–73) was appointed animal painter to the King of Hanover, and contributed 43 plates to *The Sporting Magazine*. At his best, Laporte's horses give the impression of being strong, active animals, and his backgrounds are well detailed.

One of the most striking pictures in Sally Mitchell's treasury is 'Coloured Horse in a Storm' by Charles Hancock. This is one of a pair measuring 14 x 19 in. The artist lived from 1802 to 1877, and often portrayed racehorses. He is well remembered for his series of famous winners of the Turf, and the parti-coloured horse depicted with mane and tail flying before the gale is definitely of finer type.

John Fairley's *Great Racehorses in Art* (1984) includes a small picture in black and white of a parti-coloured racehorse. The caption reads: 'By follower of George Stubbs: King George III's Racehorses (detail showing King of Trumps) c. 1790 – Sudley Art Gallery, Liverpool.' The horse appears to be a skewbald. The text reads: 'There is a picture of King George III's racehorses which includes a coloured horse, a strain completely vanished today, except on the trotting tracks.'

James Ward painted 'Horses Surprised by Wolves' in 1842. This 28¾ x 54 in. oil painting in the Tate Gallery depicts at least three skewbalds, but the intricate and

'The Travellers' by Yorkshire artists Dorothy and Elizabeth Alderson, painted in 1975.

122

'Paddling' by Malcolm Coward, oil on canvas.

sophisticated composition is not regarded as typical of his work. In 1800 Ward was commissioned by the Agricultural Society and Boydells print sellers to illustrate 200 breeds of British livestock. He did not complete the task, though some prints remain.

10 Breeding and genetics

Britain has long been known as the stud farm of the world, partly because of the soil and climate, but even more through the skill, industry and application of its breeders. Yet in the field of breeding broken-coloured horses we are far behind the USA. In Britain, we refer to a black and white broken-coloured horse or pony as a 'piebald', whether we see it out hunting, as a child's pony, drawing a gypsy caravan or parading as a drum horse in front of the Monarch. In the USA, however, it would be classified as a black *tobiano* and possibly typed.

Observation must be far more acute and detailed than at present. A careful notation of the areas and positions of colour and white, together with notation of the base colour, is extremely useful in the proper definition of a parti-coloured animal. Owners and breeders often aim for a neat and uniform fifty–fifty pattern of colour and white, but they can never be sure of getting it. What they are more likely to get are some surprises in breeding for pieds (or avoiding them)!

Carole Knowles-Pfeiffer suggests that the following be noted:

(a) the basic coat colour;
(b) the colour of the skin under the white and the non-white areas;
(c) the colour of the eyes;
(d) the *exact* location of the coloured and the white areas;
(e) the colour(s) in the mane and tail;
(f) whether there is a dorsal stripe present.

Drawings can be made of the animal, but far more accurate are clear *colour* photographs. These are usually of each side of the animal, of the head, and a view from the front and the rear. The animal should be absolutely clean and in its summer coat if possible. It improves a photograph enormously if you make the background as uncluttered as possible, and stand the animal on firm ground where its feet are clearly visible. Try to get the light slightly to one side from behind, and get in as close as you can. Fill the viewfinder, but don't cut off the nose, ears, feet or tail!

The whole subject of horse coat colour genetics bristles with difficulties. People even disagree on what constitutes a 'piebald' or a 'skewbald' – and these names are really only familiar in Britain. Referring to the rules of registration of broken-

A good, clear picture of the animal standing on firm ground is important for identification.

coloured horses outside Britain, we see that animals registered in the *overo* section of Pinto and Paint registries may have only a very small amount of white on the belly. Markings are accepted which in Britain would not even be considered as pied. But the *overos* registered in most international registries are certainly broken-coloured.

While referring back to the rules and regulations for entry into the registries outside Britain, one should note that *draught* blood of any kind is banned. That is not the case in Britain, and quite rightly, too. Many fine 'coloured' horses in Britain, especially the larger working and performance animals, have draught blood. Hunters, show jumpers, and the very useful vanner type spring to mind. Shire, Clydesdale, and Irish Draught are used a great deal and can result in superb animals for work and show purposes. Thus, while Britain has a lot to learn from overseas societies, maybe we can teach them something also.

An interesting and controversial observation by Carole Knowles-Pfeiffer is that, in some rare cases, the commonest pieds in Britain (the *tobiano*) may, in fact, be solid colour.

It is the only possible explanation for some of the breeding results I have gathered, yet it would seem to break the generally accepted 'rules of inheritance': that this pattern not only has to have one parent at least that is obviously broken-coloured, and that if the code for this pattern is present in an animal it will *always* be visible. It is supposed never to miss a generation. The question is, can it? I think that in some cases it can. And in saying this, I am blowing all accepted theories right out of the window. Actually, it can be explained genetically, but the explanation may not have very much appeal to some prominent international geneticists.

In reality, it is not so surprising when one considers the varied and often quite unexpected results one can obtain when breeding with and for coloured horses and ponies. It never ceases to surprise me, and I hate to be asked to predict the outcome of a mating; only a probable outcome. Broken-coloured horses of the *tobiano* (and *overo*) pattern can vary enormously from almost solid colour to almost pure white, and still, incidentally, be acceptable in overseas colour registries. The same must come in Britain. I think it is a fair comment that fifty–fifty colour and white is most preferred, but one can never be sure of getting it.

A pied crossed with a solid colour cannot be relied upon to produce 100% unless it carries a pied gene from *both* parents – and you just don't know by looking. A pied with one solid parent can never be stated to throw 100% pied foals. This fits in nicely with widely held genetic theory.

On the other hand, a pied mated to a pied, even if both pieds have an extended background of pied, can still produce a solid colour. This too, can be explained by genetic theory. At the same time, and in direct contrast to what I

A well-bred coloured mare visiting a Thoroughbred stud.

have just said, the Americans have very successfully bred broken-coloured animals to 15/16th and even 31/32 parts pied 'Arabian'; virtually pure bred. They have done the same with many breeds. If they can do it, so can we in Britain. It just requires knowledge and application. It should be remembered that while it is convenient to think that breeding for broken colour is relatively easy in the *tobiano* (and in most cases it is), broken colour is genetically almost certainly the result of more than one simple factor. Many factors could be involved, not just a possible basic 'pattern' factor, but also various 'additive' factors that are responsible for the enormous variations in colours/white distribution. If pattern factors are mixed, and this can be so easy if carried but unseen factors are involved, the final outcome may well be most unexpected and even unwanted. One may end up with a genetic 'soup' for extended white that results in pieds from generations of solids in breeds that ban extended white. We have a great deal to learn about this subject and a lot of honest information to be gathered.

Breeding broken coloured horses and ponies is, and may always be, largely trial and error, but the more we *know* the more we can apply to breed what we want. Good conformation and temperament usually make for a useful performer. The

Conformation and temperament must be taken into account as well as colour if a performance horse is to be produced. Louise Kerr competing cross country.

performance of a coloured horse is very much easier for most British people to judge than is its conformation. Break up the body shape, and many supposedly good judges of the horse are totally confused. Could that be partly why broken colours rarely win anything in open showing classes?

Genetics

The study of breeding has fascinated mankind since he first domesticated stock and had some control over its matings. Drawings by early cavemen appear to be an attempt at geneological tables showing extended pedigrees diagrammatically.

People who live close to their stock over long periods absorb considerable knowledge about them. Not until Mendel's 1865 experiments was there any real progress in tabulating breeding results mathematically and scientifically, and even then Mendel's work was not recognised until 1900. Yet livestock had been changed and generally improved since medieval times, without the benefits of science. Why then do we need to understand the theory of breeding now? Mike Scott, geneticist at the Animal Health Trust, Newmarket, shares his opinions and knowledge.

The answer is to save time, for thirty years is a high proportion of a human's working life, yet covers in the horse's case not more than seven or eight generations, and probably many fewer. Trial and error alone take far too long.

Genes are the basis of inheritance. They have a definite physical existence, but can be thought of as carrying 'a set of instructions' about the transmitted characteristics: hair length, size, density of bone, eye colour, and many more. These genes are strung together on chromosomes. The *locus* (plural, *loci*) describes where a particular gene occurs on a chromosome.

Every individual has two sets of genes. One set comes from the sire, the other from the dam, and both have equal value. Thus any particular function in the body is affected by two genes, one from each parent. If these genes are the same, the animal is *homozygous* or pure for that factor. If the genes are different, it is *heterozygous*.

A crucial factor to understand at this point is that the alternative forms of any particular gene do not always have the same 'strength'. One is said to be 'dominant' to the other, which is 'recessive'. An example in man is eye colour: the brown-eyed gene is dominant to the blue-eyed gene, which is recessive. As most breeders know, the bay gene is dominant to the chestnut gene, which is recessive. The practical breeder can be greatly helped by understanding these basic facts. If a foal has

The foal is born with all its potential in place: Dallas Bright Spark at one week old (*opposite page*) and (*below*) as a young stallion of 16.2 hands.

The influence of the dam and the sire are genetically equal. Royal (*right*) is by Trooper (*opposite page*) and out of Queenie (*below*). Royal now runs with his own band of mares in Stokesley, Cleveland.

HM The Queen's piebald stallion Oberon has been widely used at stud.

received a bay gene, symbolised as 'B', from one parent and a bay gene, 'B', from the other, it will be bay in colour and homozygous or pure for that colour. If it receives a chestnut gene, symbolised as 'b', from one parent and a bay gene 'B' from the other, it will be bay, because bay is dominant to chestnut, but it will be a heterozygous or impure bay (Bb). In appearance or phenotype it will be indistinguishable from a homozygous bay. The colour will be neither paler nor less lasting. Yet the animal will breed differently, and any breeder of parti-coloured horses will benefit and save valuable time if he or she understands this fact.

When 'b' meets 'b', there is no dominance; there is no bay gene to 'interfere', and the animal is chestnut, i.e. without black points.

There are several sets of genes controlling coat colour, but in most horses, including bays, chestnuts and greys, there are only three or four genes that need to be considered when looking at colour. An animal will carry the bay and/or chestnut genes, and elsewhere on the same or other chromosomes carry the genes for grey, the genes for black and the genes for 'colouring'. Other genes may have 'modifying' influences, for example dun or buckskin.

The 'A' gene is a geneticist's term for the gene that controls the distribution of black hair over the body. In its 'A' form the gene confines the black to the points – the lower legs, the mane and the tail. But it can only operate in conjunction with the 'B' gene that 'instructs' for the production of black hair pigment. It could not do so if there was no black to operate on. Its effect is to produce a bay (by definition with black points) as opposed to a black.

The 'A' gene's alternative is the 'a' gene. This does not restrict the distribution of black hair over the body. Therefore, again in conjunction with the 'B' gene, it produces a uniformly black horse. However, since 'a' is recessive to 'A', a true black horse can only be produced when 'a' is inherited from both parents, i.e. the animal is homozygous for black. The combination Aa (in conjunction with 'B') will produce a bay horse.

In the grey, the 'G' gene instructs the pigment to be lost progressively from the tip of the hair down to the base. As horse people know, grey foals are often born fully pigmented. They gradually lose the pigment from the tips of the hairs, but not from the skin. It is like a man going grey; he loses the colour of his hair, but not the colour of his scalp.

In the roan, white and coloured hairs are intermixed. Sometimes roan coloration and grey are confused, but the genetic control of roan is quite separate from the grey genes; it is vital to appreciate this fact. A 'blue' roan carries a mixture of dark and white hairs; it is born that way, and remains that way. Unlike the grey, it does not become lighter with age. A 'strawberry roan' is a mixture of red (chestnut) and white hairs. In English usage a red roan is a mixture of bay and white hairs, and has black points. In the USA only red roan (bay or chestnut) and blue roan are recognised.

If the grey factor is understood, it becomes easier for the breeder of parti-coloured horses to apply the knowledge to his or her own programme. Inheritance of the grey factor illustrates Mendel's law very well. If a homozygous grey is mated with a horse of another colour, no matter what, all the individuals in the first cross-bred generation will be grey.

The grey Arabian stallion Amurath in Hanover sired 900 foals out of mares of every colour, but including very few grey mares. Every single foal was a grey. If Amurath had been heterozygous for grey, half his foals from the non-grey mares would have been expected to be grey, and half non-grey. If these non-greys were mated together, not a single grey would be born. Scientists, breeders and students of stud books all agree that for a grey to be born, one of the parents must be grey, because grey is dominant to non-grey.

Similarly, tobiano is dominant to non-tobiano (i.e. solid colour). As with grey, the colour pattern appears to be controlled by a single dominant gene. A homozygous tobiano (picture the white poured down from the top) will when mated to horses of any other colour produce 100 per cent broken coloured foals. A current practical example is HM The Queen's Oberon, standing at the Cuba Stud, Malton, North Yorkshire. Oberon is piebald, part-bred Dutch by Orleander out of Juniper, and registered with the Painted Horse and Pony Society of Great Britain. Oberon's stud card guardedly claims that he has thrown only coloured foals to date. If after such extended use he began to throw solid colours, it would indeed upset genetic theory. But he has not, and it is almost safe to say that he cannot. HM The Queen's red and white stallion Mars has similar characteristics.

We have seen that it is most helpful to know if the horse is homozygous or heterozygous for the colour pattern, and this can be proven in one of two ways.

Though the dam's influence is equal to that of the stallion in each offspring, she seldom has enough foals to prove mathematically that she is homozygous. If she is a tobiano and has had ten tobiano foals, that would suggest that she is homozygous, but twenty or more would really be needed for positive conclusions, and that is an unrealistic number. The stallion, on the other hand, could readily sire more than that number in a single season. A conclusion could be made a year later.

The other method is by blood-typing the albumin. It appears that the tobiano gene is very closely linked to the albumin gene on the chromosome, and is inherited with it. The albumin can be readily typed by an equine blood-typing laboratory. It would be a major step forward if parti-coloured stallions were blood-typed in this way, and careful records kept of the colour of all progeny.

Less is known about the overo pattern, but its genetic control is different from tobiano. A further complication is that the tobiano and the overo pattern may appear on the same animal. There are still huge gaps in our knowledge, despite study by scientists and breeders. White in the overo pattern comes up ventrally (from below), and seems linked to very white legs and white belly.

Most breeders would prefer to use a parti-coloured stallion as near as possible to the conformation, colour and markings of the type they favoured. But as yet we are unable to control the pattern or even the proportion of colour to white.

People new to coloured horse breeding sometimes ask: 'If all four grandparents are parti-coloured, but the parents are not, does that raise the chances of parti-colouring offspring?' The answer is definitely *no*. Alluding once more to the grey, heterozygous greys bred together would produce on average one non-grey and three greys, two of the latter being heterozygous and one homozygous. The non-greys mated together would never produce a grey, nor would the non-parti-coloureds (i.e. solid colours) produce a parti-colour. Neither with greys nor parti-coloureds is any difference in appearance observable between homozygotes and

Libran Luck, registered with HIS and Weatherbys. A tobiano mare who has produced the tobiano stallion Dallas Bright Spark.

heterozygotes. The effect of a dominant gene is by definition always seen; the effect of a recessive is not. A horse may have four bay grandparents yet be a chestnut. This is because at least two of those grandparents were heterozygous bay, carrying the chestnut (recessive) gene which was hidden. When the recessive chestnut gene meets another recessive chestnut, there is no dominant bay involved, and the offspring is a chestnut.

A heterozygous tobiano would on average have equal chances of throwing broken-coloured and whole-coloured foals from whole-coloured mares. This probability is based on the same statistics that govern the tossing of a coin. A tossed coin is expected to land an equal number of heads and tails over a reasonable number of attempts. If the coin lands 'heads' four times in succession, that is not too rare. If it falls 'heads' more than, say, ten times in succession, there is probably something odd about the coin, i.e. it is double-headed. In terms of the tobiano gene, it is pure or homozygous for that factor. Carry on throwing heads in twenty throws, and the matter is virtually clinched.

A stud farm owner of long experience observed that, if parti-coloureds are bred together for a number of generations, the colour becomes gradually less distinct and its proportion smaller. We may note this while remembering that there are as yet no controlled experiments to back it up. As gypsies and travelling people often introduce a solid colour into their parti-coloured strains, this does seem a sensible move if the foals start coming too light. In the present state of our knowledge, we cannot be dogmatic about it. One idea would be to mate a homozygous tobiano with a solid-coloured partner of the desired hue, whether bay, black, grey or chestnut. The aim would be a parti-coloured foal with the colour fraction intense and well-defined. By recording all such matings and progeny with the coloured horse societies, our sum of knowledge would be considerably enlarged. In the overo pattern, there is more merging of white and the other colours, and even a certain amount of mottling.

Though breeding of colour is and will always remain a fascinating exercise, it is only one aspect of the programme. The prettiest colours are of no use without sound limbs and joints, the required bone and substance, action whether for driving, riding or jumping and, among many other factors, equable temperament.

On no account must coloured horse people follow the path trodden by so many breeders in so many classes of domesticated livestock and pets, and make colour markings their only goal. That road can lead only to disaster.

Bibliography

Apsley, Lady Viola. *Bridleways through History*. Hutchinson, 1936 rev. edn 1948

Bagnold, Enid. *National Velvet*. Penguin Books, 1935

Carter, Major General William Harding. *Horses of the World*. National Geographic Society, 1923

Chivers, Keith. *The Shire Horse*. J. A. Allen, 1976

De Trafford, H. *Horses of the British Empire*. Southwood, 1908

Dent, Anthony. *Donkey: The Story of the Ass from East to West*. George Harrap, 1972

Dobie, J. Frank. *The Mustangs*. Bramhall House, New York, 1934

English Cart-Horse Society Stud Book, Vol. I, 1880

Ewart, Prof. J. Cosser. Various writings

Fairley, John. *Great Racehorses in Art*. 1984

Fitzgerald, Brian Vesey. *Gypsies of Britain*. Chapman & Hall, 1944

Gay, Carl W. *Productive Horse Husbandry*. Lippincott Farm Manuals, 1913

Gilbey, Sir Walter. *Horses: Breeding to Colour*. Vinton, 1907

Mackenzie, R. W. R. *Standard Cyclopedia of Modern Agriculture*. Gresham, 1908

Mirus, Ilse. 'The legend of the odd-coloured horses', from *Hufschlag Erklang*, 1960, translated by Daphne Machin Goodall in *The Horseman's Companion*, ed. Dorian Williams, Eyre & Spottiswoode, 1967

Mitchell, Sally. *Dictionary of British Equestrian Artists*, 1985

Moses, J. W. *Mustangs and Cow Horses*, 1940

Pocock, Roger. *Horses*. J. Murray, 1917

Richardson, Clive. *The Fell Pony*. J. A. Allen, 1990

Russell, Valerie. *Heavy Horses of the World*. Country Life, 1983

Ryder, Tom. *The High Stepper*, J. A. Allen, 1961

Seaby, Allan W. *Skewbald the New Forest Pony*. 1923 (*Sheltie: The Story of a Shetland Pony*, 1924

Shetland Pony Stud-book Society. Centenary Edition magazine, 1990

Somerville, E. Œ. and Ross, Martin. *Some Experiences of an Irish RM*. 1901 *Further Experiences of an Irish RM*. 1908

Sponenberg, D. Phillip and Beaver, Bonnie V. *Horse Color*. Texas A & M University Press, 1983

Stuart, Lord David. *An Illustrated History of Belted Cattle*. Scottish Academic
  Press, 1970
Suffolk Horse Society Stud Book, Vol. I. 1880
Swinfen, Lady Averil. *The Irish Donkey*. Mercia Press, Dublin, 1969
    Donkeys Galore! David & Charles, 1976
Tesio, Frederico. *Breeding the Racehorse*. J. A. Allen, 1958
Walker, Stella. *Sporting Art: England 1700–1900*. Studio Vista, 1972
Wentworth, Lady. *The World's Best Horse*. Allen & Unwin, 1958
Williams, Dorian. *The Classical Riding Master*. Eyre Methuen, 1979

Index

144